Praise

WE CAN ^ LIVE GREEN
ALL

"Very empowering information, presented in a thoughtful and well organized way. *WE CAN (ALL) LIVE GREEN* shows how simple it is to be good to ourselves and the Earth by our everyday choices. Make a difference and take it to the bank!

— **Hugo and Debra Saavedra**
Co-founders, Hugo Naturals

"If you're looking to save money and do the right thing, or you'd like to know more about the story behind the things you buy, read this book. Jennifer Noonan takes the mystery out of going green and living green. Written simply and clearly for today's eco-minded consumer."

— **Mary Bemis**
Co-founder and Editor-in-Chief, Organic Spa Magazine

"This is a terrific reference that connects all the positive aspects of green living, including the often-overlooked cost-savings factor. The book clearly outlines how simple lifestyle changes have direct positive benefits for the planet, your health and your wallet (how soon can I start!)."

— **Elizabeth Borelli**
Founder of Nubius Organics (and sustainability evangelist)

"Jennifer Noonan has accomplished something rare and very timely: the seminal book on living an environmentally friendly lifestyle. Using great wit and wisdom, she gives us information that will inspire and empower anyone to make green a way of life. WE CAN (ALL) LIVE GREEN provides an easy-to-navigate roadmap to a healthier life for us and for our planet."

— Racquel Palmese
Managing Editor, Green Technology

"*WE CAN (ALL) LIVE GREEN* offers great projects designed for anyone on a modest budget who wants to help turn things around – simple, low cost, easy-to-carry-out projects that could make a huge difference in the way we live. Unlike a lot of today's "green" literature, its also well-written and not at all preachy!"

— Dickson Despommier, Ph.D.
Professor of Environmental Health Sciences, Columbia University

WE CAN ^ LIVE GREEN

ALL

WE CAN *ALL* LIVE GREEN

SIMPLE STEPS TO SAVE MONEY, STAY HEALTHY,
AND SUPPORT THE PLANET

Jennifer Noonan

St. lynn's
press

PITTSBURGH

We Can (all) Live Green
Simple Steps to Save Money, Stay Healthy and Support Our Planet

ISBN-13: 978-0-9800288-2-9

Library of Congress Control Number: 2008924172
CIP information available upon request

First Edition, 2008

St. Lynn's Press . POB 18680 . Pittsburgh, PA 15236
412.466.0790 • www.stlynnspress.com

Typesetting—Holly Wensel, Network Printing Services
Cover design—Jeff Nicoll
Editor—Catherine Dees

Printed in the United States of America
on recycled paper ✪

This title and all of St. Lynn's Press books may be purchased for educational, business, or sales promotional use. For information please write:

Special Markets Department, St. Lynn's Press,
POB 18680, Pittsburgh, PA 15236

10 9 8 7 6 5 4 3 2 1

Table of Contents

❀

Note to the Reader

Forget going green. Forget climate change. Forget peak oil and rising food costs. Focus for a moment on the following three questions:

Would you like to save money?
Would you like to improve your health?
Would you like to support your community, the nation and the planet?

If you answered yes to any of these, then this book was written for you.

In the following pages I'm going to show you how you can make small changes in your everyday life that will add up to a big difference in your health and the planet's health – without breaking your budget. In fact, you'll learn how you can save a fair chunk of change and make some money in the process. It's all about arming yourself with knowledge and strategies.

———————

We live in a time when our lives are moving at light speed and we're bombarded daily with major issues that affect our future. You know what they are, I don't have to tell you – the ailing economy at home, worries about job loss, not to mention food shortages abroad and climate change everywhere... How do we even *begin* to address what's wrong?

We want to do the right thing, but how do we fit saving the world into the never-ending merry-go-round of work and home responsibilities? By the end of the day we're exhausted. Add to that the increasing squeeze on our pocketbooks, and it's easy to feel there's nothing we can do to hoist ourselves – let alone the world – out of the situations we face. And if someone says to us, "Going green is a big step in the right direction," our response is likely to be, "Nope, can't afford it...much as I'd like to."

You're just the person I wrote this book for. As a public school teacher and a new mom, I know from personal experience that living green is possible on a tight budget. I am all too familiar with the constant struggle between making the bills, doing the right thing and trying to create a future for my family. That is why I will be giving you not only the why's and how's, but lots and lots of cost comparisons, buying strategies and creative alternatives. These days, there's no substitute for smart and savvy.

I'm going to provide you with some easy-to-use tools that focus on three key areas of our lives – money, health and community – that are in dire need of a little attention. In the pages that follow, you will find attainable ways to put more money in your pocketbook (I promise!), improve your health and support your community – all as a result of making good, informed choices and doing the right thing.

What's Inside

Inside, you'll find action items and suggestions for every aspect of your daily activities – products you can count on and ones to avoid; less expensive alternatives to everything, from what you eat to how you get to work; safer products for your home; projects you can create alone or with your family, or in your school or workplace. Icons, call-out boxes, science-in-a-nutshell factoids and other features will help draw your attention to important tips and topics – as well as their level of cost, health implications and eco-friendliness.

Take it to the bank! At the end of almost every section you'll discover a **Take It to the Bank** summary that totals the cash savings you can achieve by implementing even a few of the recommended strategies for that area of your lifestyle. We don't just talk a good talk about saving you money, we show you exactly what you can look forward to. You're going to be pleasantly surprised.

What else? In the Appendix, you'll find a Simple Science section that explores some of the underlying scientific principles; as well as a helpful glossary of terms – it's a whole new world out there, so you've got to learn the lingo that goes with it. And finally, a book like this wouldn't be complete without a list of recommended resources for products and services.

It's all here, awaiting your discovery of a new and better way to live in harmony with this incredibly beautiful Earth of ours. I hope the information in We Can (all) Live Green helps you to improve your finances, your family's health and your community. Along the way, you'll be doing the right thing for the planet too. A win-win-win.

You can do it! Keep reading to find out how!

Jennifer Noonan

ICONS

One of the most useful icons in the book will be (🌱) . Whenever you see this symbol of a hopeful sapling sprouting up from the earth, it's telling you how much green value a particular product or project has...how much you and the planet will benefit from the time, effort or money expended. This sapling is part of the logo for our online guide to all things green, **wecanlivegreen.com**.

Another icon you'll be seeing a lot of is the dollar sign. This will show you the relative cost of a product or project, and sometimes it will indicate the level of money that you will be saving instead of spending.

Example: If a recommended purchase or project has icons after it that look like this: (🌱🌱🌱 and $$), you can expect that for a moderate initial cost ($$) you will reap a substantial eco-benefit (🌱🌱🌱) – in health, environmental benefit and cash savings down the road.

Why What You Buy Matters

Here's a little secret: As a consumer in our consumer-driven world, you have the power. It's true. You choose to buy – or not to buy. Right now, all across the globe, marketing analysts, advertising firms and top-level CEOs of billion dollar companies are poring over graphs and charts to find out what you spend your money on. *"Me? Little old me?"* you ask. Absolutely! Believe it or not, you control the consumer marketplace. What you choose to spend your money on drives companies to make more (or less) of a product, or completely change the way they make it.

> ☞ *In the U.S. alone, total media advertising in 2006 was over **281 billion dollars**. That number includes the cost of consumer research focus groups studying what you buy and why, marketing strategies created just for you, and advertising fine-tuned to your specific inclinations.*

After you digest the fact that a whole lot of people are actually paying attention to what you buy every day, you might be filled with a sense of...well, **power**. However, many of us may not feel so powerful right now due to the state of the economy and the falling dollar. Recent economic changes in our nation have forced many of us to reevaluate our financial situation and analyze what we spend our money on – and ask ourselves how we can change our habits so we can get the best out of tighter times, and still be able to do the right thing for our families and our communities.

I'm here to offer you lots of help in the area of saving money and doing the right thing. Before we get to that though, let's take a quick look at the products we buy – where they come from, how they get to us and where they go when we're done with them.

> ☞ *The U.S. is 5% of the global population – but we use 30% of the global resources. (We really do have a lot of stuff!)*

STORY TIME: The lifecycle of stuff

Every product has a story, yet we as the consumers see only a small part of it, the part that's packaged and advertised with us in mind. But there's so much more we should know about it. By the time the product gets to us, it has already been on a very long journey, not just in miles but in processing, and that is part of what is getting our planet in trouble, not to mention our health. Recent alarming headlines about lead paint in our children's toys and toxic chemicals in our household products have prompted us to ask more questions about where our products come from and what goes into them – and ultimately, into the environment and into our bodies.

The truth is, products in the marketplace today are far more likely to harm the environment than to help it, or even be neutral. **But on a positive note:** New, greener products are becoming available that leave less of a "footprint" on the planet, which is a step in the right direction – and *this* is why the media and everyone else is so excited about greener products. They aren't a perfect solution. But they're better. And on an even greener note, these healthier choices can actually help you save money!

The basic life story of a product goes something like this: The raw materials to make the product are extracted (harvested from natural resources), then the raw materials are put together to create the product and its packaging (production). Then it is distributed to stores where it can be purchased. Then the consumer buys the product, takes it home and uses it. Last, the product is disposed of.

In each step there are choices that can be made to help or harm the environment. How many natural resources will be used? How will they be extracted from the environment? What types of chemicals will be used? Will the production cause air and water pollution? How will the product be made and packaged? How will the waste from making it be disposed of? How will the product itself be disposed of when we're finished with it?

FOOTPRINT? WHAT FOOTPRINT?

You may be saying to yourself. "I don't like to think I'm having a negative effect on the environment. I've been recycling my bottles and cans for years." And that's a very good thing, but unless you also know the story behind the products you are using, you might be buying items that have a less than ideal environmental impact. For most of these products there are safer and often cheaper alternatives available to you. You just need to know that they exist (my job!) and that it's possible to do the planet a huge favor at the same time as you're helping your own bottom line.

There are all sorts of websites out there that will tell you about your carbon footprint and your environmental footprint, based on your buying and consumption profile (everything from food to transportation to home heating and cooling). Ultimately, it is tough to pin down a definite percentage contribution that each of us makes to the big, not-so-happy state of our planet.

Case in point: As this book goes to press there is news that our LCD flat-screen displays contain a chemical that is a potent greenhouse gas, nitrogen trifluoride, or NF_3. It is **17,000 times stronger than CO_2**. NF_3s are poised to dramatically affect Earth's climate because of soaring demand for flat-screen TVs. In Chapter 9 we will see that plasma TVs are also energy vampires, but now we're seeing that that's just half the story!

Now what? What are you supposed to do...stop buying stuff and go live in bearskins in the woods? That doesn't make sense. But neither does continuing to support products and practices that are hurting our environment and yes, hurting all of *us*! If you know more about the story behind the things you buy and use, you'll have more ammunition to make smart and savvy consumer choices, at the same time as you're saving money – **real, take-it-to-the-bank money**.

So let's start with something close to all our hearts: food.

Part One

You and Your Food

The Goal: Consuming the least possible amounts of pesticides, artificial additives and other dangerous contaminants found in foods. Supporting healthy, sustainable farming and diary practices. Staying within the family's food budget despite rising costs.

The Reality: Contaminants are in most of the foods we normally consume, and those foods are often cheaper than organic, pesticide-free or partially organic food products. But not always, and that's where the strategy comes in. See below.

The Strategy: Knowing which foods it's worth spending a little extra to avoid (the highly contaminated ones), and which you don't have to worry too much about if you're watching your pennies. Knowing how (and where) to "buy smart": alternatives to supermarket produce, buying local, farmers markets, co-ops, etc. Knowing (and actively using) the tips in this book to save you money on food.

I Eat, Therefore I Am

All living things need four things to survive: food, water, air and shelter. That's it!

We love food for many reasons – primarily because we need it to survive. But enjoying food is also a complex psychological, chemical and emotional process. It feels good to eat. Eating is associated with other pleasurable activities, like spending time with family and friends. The fact is, certain types of food (fatty, fried, rich, or sugary foods) make our taste buds happy, but not the rest of our body. It's something to keep in mind as we move through this chapter. Many of our food choices are based on what our taste buds dictate, instead of what our body actually needs. Can you "educate" your taste buds to demand healthier food? Yes, indeed.

Science Fact
You have 10,000 taste buds in your mouth and between 10,000,000,000,000 and 100,000,000,000,000 (that's trillions!) cells in your body. Which should you be listening to? Hmmm.

Fortunately for most of us, we do have choices – we make them every day. So let's start by asking a few pertinent questions.

WHAT'S IN MY FOOD BESIDES FOOD?

Most of our food that sits on our grocery shelves has a very long story to tell. And the longer a food product's story, the more we wind up paying for it – in dollars and cents, in health problems, in environmental cost, or a little of each. All food starts out in one of four ways: by means of farming, raising livestock, hunting or fishing. While some foods can be eaten raw (think fruits and veggies), most raw food materials undergo a specific process to create a food product (think juice, pasta and snacks). Many foods start their life cycle on a farm, where pesticides and other chemicals are used to control insects and increase crop production. These traditional agricultural methods have come under increased scrutiny as we learn more about chemicals and how chemicals interact with the human body. Questions have been raised: Just how much of a pesticide (or herbicide) – which in most cases is toxic to humans – is passed on to humans through our food? How do these chemicals affect the human body when we ingest them?

 Science Fact
Since World War II, over 100,000 man-made chemicals have been created, only 10,000 of which have been tested for their effects on the human body.

Why are chemicals such as pesticides bad for us? The chemicals in the cells of our body interact with chemicals in the food we eat, the air we breathe and the water we drink. Some chemicals interact well with our body – they may even help our body to work more efficiently. Others have an opposite effect and are very harmful – even toxic – and can do serious damage to the cells of our body. (For some in-a-nutshell facts about chemicals and your body, check out the Simple Science section in the Appendix.)

Because I'm not fond of strange chemicals in my food any more than you are, I want to tell you about an alternative way to produce food. It's how all foods used to be back in our grandparents' day. Back before all those man-made chemicals started coming into our food chain and our bodies. Nobody was using the word "organic" to refer to our table food, because they didn't have to. Organic was just the way Nature gave it to us. So, here's some basic information about organic foods.

ORGANIC, PURE AND SIMPLE

An organic product is simply a product that has not been grown using chemical pesticides, synthetic fertilizers or a host of other methods – i.e., *bioengineering* (this includes growth hormones, antibiotics and genetically modified organisms) and radiation (including ionizing radiation).*

Most organic foods currently cost a bit more because organic farming methods are more labor- and time-intensive. Conventional agriculture uses easier, "quick" methods such as pesticides and soil depleting mono-crop farming – so the immediate cost of produce grown that way might be lower, but the long term costs in health and environmental degradation are eventually paid for by you and me. Ironically, when you buy organic you're paying for what's not in your food (pesticides, herbicides, hormones, etc).

---

* See Glossary for definitions

Think of it as the cheapest kind of preventive health care, because that's exactly what it is: Buying organic adds up to overall reduction in health care costs over time, due to lower exposures to toxic chemicals for you and your family. But how does a family in today's economy change their food purchasing habits to make room for organic? Hold that thought while I tell you a bit more about it…and then get to the solutions for you.

> *Organic products have experienced a 17 to 20% growth rate over the last several years. The rapid growth numbers mean that lower consumer prices won't be far behind, because the entire market sector is expanding, and the laws of economics are coming into play. When Wal-Mart hops on the organics bandwagon, can others be far behind?*

Organically grown food reduces the amount of pesticides, insecticides and other harmful chemicals in our environment. This means fewer harmful chemicals in your food, your water and everywhere else you spend time!

Think about it: If frogs and fish are starting to mutate from the toxic stuff we've allowed to flow into our waterways, how smart is it for Homo sapiens (that's us, folks!) to just keep doing what we've been doing?

In the U. S., organic food is regulated by the U.S. Department of Agriculture. Organic farms must strictly adhere to guidelines and rules on organic farming. The USDA Organic Seal ensures that the product meets organic standards. A product must have the USDA Organic seal to be labeled organic. Also, an accredited certifying agency needs to certify the product as organic. There are 97 Accredited Certifying Agents (56 domestic and 41 foreign) that certify the product as organic.

The USDA Organic Seal

Because government regulations are never simple and straightforward, there are now at least three categories of certified organic:

- **100% organic** – Must contain 100% organic ingredients, not including added water or salt. (Can be labeled "100% organic" and display the USDA seal)

- **95% organic** – Must contain 95% organic ingredients, not including added water or salt. Must not contain sulfites. May contain up to 5% of non-organically grown ingredients. (Can be labeled "organic" and display the USDA seal)

- **70% organic** – May contain 70% of organic ingredients, not including added water or salt. May contain 30% non-organic ingredients (the label can read, "Made with organic ingredients" but it can't display the USDA organic seal).

- **Less than 70% organic** – The label might read, "Contains less than 70% organic ingredients" and/or list the organic ingredients that it does contain.

Organic food products are somewhat more expensive, depending on where you live and shop. But sometimes there can be pleasant surprises: Recently in Los Angeles, 99 Cents Only stores were carrying organic cherry tomatoes, hearts of romaine, Sun-Maid dried apricots, Hershey's chocolate bars, Sargento mozzarella and Pillsbury frozen pie crust. **All organic** and all under a dollar.

Most estimates note a difference in the price of organics versus traditional food at between 5% and 40%. But those are broad averages – there are lots of local alternatives where organics are even cheaper than supermarket non-organics. Organic fruits and vegetables, for instance, will almost always be significantly cheaper at farmers markets, U-picks, co-ops and CSAs – which I'll tell you all about later in this chapter. The most important thing right now is not to think "expensive!" and completely give up on organic. Below are a few recommendations for you to start integrating organic into your budget without increasing your grocery costs.

FRUITS AND VEGGIES

If you are on a tight budget, focus first on produce items that are known to contain high pesticide levels under ordinary cultivation. These are the best items to begin buying organic, because fruits and vegetables are so highly absorptive of the toxic chemicals used in the growing process. Humans in turn ingest them, which means we are constantly putting toxic chemicals into our bodies. Not good.

In 2007, the Environmental Working Group published an eye-opening study on pesticide levels in fruits and vegetables.

Here are the top 12 fruits and vegetables in both their "best" and "worst" categories. Keep this list handy for your next trip to the grocery store – it gives you an idea of what you definitely shouldn't skimp on in the organic produce department.

Dirty Dozen – buy these organic

1. Peaches
2. Apples
3. Sweet Bell Peppers
4. Celery
5. Nectarines
6. Strawberries
7. Cherries
8. Lettuce
9. Grapes (Imported)
10. Pears
11. Spinach
12. Potatoes

Cleanest 12 – lowest in pesticides

1. Onions
2. Avocado
3. Sweet Corn (Frozen)
4. Pineapples
5. Mango
6. Sweet Peas (Frozen)
7. Asparagus
8. Kiwi
9. Bananas
10. Cabbage
11. Broccoli
12. Eggplant

For the complete list of the top pesticide-carrying fruit and veggie culprits, check our Resources Appendix for the Environmental Working Group's Food News division.

Not Organic, But Getting There

Besides certified organic, there are many levels of healthy, chemical-free food options out there for you. Here's a quick rundown of terms to look for in your food shopping – especially when shopping at local farmers markets, co-ops, etc:

Certified Organic: *Government regulated farming in which the environment is not harmed. The focus is improved soil fertility as well as farm sustainability.*

Naturally Grown: *A farm that does not have an organic certification, but follows organic principles in farming techniques. Many smaller farms have the "naturally grown" label as the USDA organic certification process is very expensive and not all small farms can afford this expense.*

Certified Naturally Grown: *A certification program specifically for farmers that sell locally and directly to customers.*

Transitional: *A farm that is working towards organic certification, but has yet to complete the years-long process of organic certification.*

Conventional: *This does not necessarily include traditional large-scale chemical agriculture. Conventional farms are typically smaller farms that sparingly use chemicals on their crops as needed.*

Biodynamic: *A non-chemical movement that focuses on harnessing the biological systems of nature to ensure healthy produce.*

(Source: Local Harvest.org)

MILK PRODUCTS

Once you have incorporated organic produce into your grocery bill, you can turn your attention to dairy items (butter, cheese, milk, etc). These products are made from animal breast milk, which comes from the fatty tissue of the animal. Fatty tissue, most specifically breast milk, is where many persistent toxins build up in the body of any living animal. Animal milk is what gives us cheese, milk and butter, so if you are drinking non-organic milk, you and your family are taking in higher levels of these toxins (including antibiotics and hormones) than if you drank organic milk.

Nice to know: Wal-Mart now offers milk that is free of artificial growth hormones, its Great Value brand – which is a budget friendly possibility for you to keep in mind, if you still buy non-organic milk. So why did Wal-Mart decide to offer this hormone-free milk? Customer demand, pure and simple.

Also, consider trying non-animal products such as **soy milk, soy cheese**, etc. These options are typically cheaper than their animal product counterparts, and you don't have to worry about growth hormones and antibiotics in your food. Soy products are good sources of protein and other nutrients, with **well-documented** health benefits.

> ☞ *From 2007 to 2008 the price of milk soared 30% and is expected to rise over the coming years due to increased demand for milk globally, increased feed prices, as well as higher energy and transportation costs.*

As of this writing:

1 gallon of milk = **$4.00** on average (some places on the East and West Coast charge closer to **$7.00** a gallon!)

1 gallon of soy milk = Less than **$3.00** on average (leading brands are usually generous with coupons.)

If you give soy milk a try, you are saving at least a dollar over a gallon of milk – and more like $3.00 in some places. With rising gas prices, that extra $3.00 sure might come in handy somewhere else in the budget!

MEATS

Next step, start to switch your meats and chicken and turkey to **organic, free-range** and **hormone-free**. The benefits to your health are huge. If your budget can't manage the added cost, consider a few organic non-meat options such as tofu, soy products or lentils, to supplement or take the place of a typical meat meal (see our vegetarian section below...and see Chapter 3). It's a fact, you don't have to have meat with every meal to get your RDA of protein. As you will see, not eating meat at every meal – while still getting your RDA of protein – can mean big savings for your pocketbook.

> ☞ *The Recommended Daily Allowance of protein for an adult male is 60 grams, slightly less for an adult female. For children, the RDA varies from 13 to 36 grams, depending on age, weight and other factors.*

Some protein content comparisons:

Chicken: (4 oz. serving) 25 grams
Lean ground beef: (3 oz. serving) 23 +/- grams
Pork: (4 oz. serving) 25 grams
Firm Tofu: (4 oz. serving) 15 grams
Lentils: (4 oz. serving) 10 grams

Cost Comparisons to feed a family of 4 (16 oz. of protein):

Chicken: $6.00
Lean ground beef: $3.00
Pork: $3.50
Tofu: $2.00 (costs 75% less than chicken, 35% less than ground beef, 30% less than pork)
Lentils: $1.50 (costs 85% less than chicken, 50% less than ground beef, 60% less than pork)

Note: The above percentages are estimates only, but helpful as general comparisons.

By making a change in the type of protein you are serving, you can save close to **$5.00 per meal**. Did trying vegetarian just get a little more attractive?

If you plan ahead and make the switch slowly from non-organic to organic, all-meat to not-every-day meat, you will discover that your grocery bill will become a bit more manageable – and you will be well on your way to a healthier lifestyle. The important thing is to focus on making changes you can afford and you can stick to, as well as identifying where you can save money in the process. Remember, if you begin to put your consumer dollar towards organic products, corporations will take note and they will follow where you lead them. Wal-Mart's listening, and so are corporations everywhere!

Still not convinced? We took three separate eating plans for one day, averaged the cost per person, and got the following table. Take a look – the results might surprise you.

A Day In The Life:
How We Eat and What It Costs

Here's a snapshot of a typical day's meals and their cost — from take-out, processed, or whole foods (not the market chain). Here, "Whole foods" means more natural and close to the source.

Meal	Take-out	Processed	Whole foods
Breakfast	Coffee House Latte ($4.00) & Muffin ($2.00) — $6.00	Toaster pastries (2) with bottled cold coffee — $3.75	Scrambled Egg Sandwich — 2 eggs, 2 pieces of bread, mayo, tomato with orange juice — $2.85
Lunch	Fast Food Value Meal — $6.50 and up	Microwave Dinner — Chicken Lasagna $4.00	Turkey Burger with lettuce, tomato, pickles and mustard and organic corn chips — $2.55
Dinner	Take-out Pasta and Salad with Drink — $8.50 and up	Frozen chicken nuggets, macaroni & cheese, with pre-made green beans & almonds — $4.50	Chicken Stir fry with vegetables and brown rice — $3.25
TOTAL	**$21.00/day**	**$12.25/day**	**$8.65/day**

There it is, in black and white. Try out your own cost comparison. By the way, we didn't factor in the savings in health care costs and future medical bills for the whole foods diet — that would put your savings literally off the chart!

Chips

Whole Foods: (Organic Barbeque) $2.39
Trader Joe's: (Organic Corn) $1.99
Albertsons: (Doritos) $3.50
             (Cheetos) $2.49
             (Lay's) $4.00
Wal-Mart: (Cheetos) $3.50

Cookies

Whole Foods: (Organic Chocolate Chip Soft Cookies) $3.49
Trader Joe's: (Chocolate Chip Soft Cookies) $3.29
Albertsons: (Chips Ahoy) $4.29
             (Oreos Regular or Double Stuff) $3.99
Wal-Mart: (Chips Ahoy) $2.99

> ☞ ***Food fact 101:*** *When you eat better, your body is less prone to cravings and insatiable hunger because you are giving it the vitamins, minerals and nutrition it needs in order to run well.*

HELP! THEY DON'T SELL ORGANIC PRODUCE IN MY LOCAL GROCERY STORE!

No need to panic. There are many other organic or close-to-organic options out there for you – most of which are even better and fresher than what your local grocery store can provide. They are by far the healthiest alternatives out there and, yes, you really can save money shopping at these places for organic produce. The next chapter will give you information about farmers markets, Community Supported Agriculture programs (CSAs) and more.

But first, why are these options better for you and your budget than a national grocery chain? **In a word: energy.** A whole lot of energy is consumed to transport foods to our neighborhood supermarket.

How Does Food Get To Me? This is as much an economic question as an environmental one, because the answer determines how much you are going to have to pay for your food. The more energy used to make and deliver a product, the more expensive it will be. Part of the reason we've seen skyrocketing food prices lately is transportation costs, which respond to soaring fuel costs. It's all related, and ultimately you, the consumer, pay the price. Generally speaking, the realities are these:

- The less energy used to produce our food the better, and

- The more energy used to create a product, the more the consumer will have to pay for it (not to mention the environment).

Now I want to talk about the value of buying and eating foods that haven't traveled a long distance to get to you – and tell you all the ways that you and the planet can benefit.

two

Buying And Eating Local

bringin' it on home

You've probably seen it on bumper stickers: "Buy Local." The idea was such a fixture in the media a while back that the New Oxford American Dictionary named "locavore" 2007's Word of the Year.

> **Locavore:** *a person who consumes food farmed and harvested within a 50, 100 or 150 mile radius of their home.*

WHY IT'S SUCH A BIG DEAL

Local food is fresh. Most produce in the U.S. is picked 4 to 7 days before it lands on a supermarket shelf and travels an average of 1,500 miles to get to you. And that's just domestic food. Imagine what it took to get those New Zealand apples or Chilean grapes here.

> ☞ *Once a fruit or veggie is picked, it immediately begins losing nutrients. This means that the longer you wait to eat that perfect pear, the fewer vitamins and minerals you'll get from it.*

Local food is better for the environment. Local foods require less packaging to stay fresh during transport. It's a lot easier to carry a tomato down the street in good shape than it is to send it half way around the world in 3 trucks, a boat and maybe a train. Of course, it will use a lot less fuel too. The term "food miles" commonly refers to how far a food item must travel in order to get to the consumer.

Local food supports your community. It just makes sense: When you buy local, you're keeping money in your community and supporting farmers who turn their profit right back into the local economy. This creates a nice little cycle of economic growth and sustainability here at home. Another benefit is that you'll have a lot more access to your food producers, so you can pick their brains about what they know best: food! Yep, you can just go talk to them. You'll get the scoop on produce availability, harvest times and what this year's harvest will yield…they may even have a few great recipes they're willing to share with you.

Local food is cheaper. Finally, did I say that local food is cheaper? Local food is cheaper. More of your hard-earned cash gets to say right in your pocket.

From a Slogan to a Habit

Buying local is easy – and can actually be fun. Here are a few of the most common options in both rural *and* urban communities. Remember, just because a local farmer does not have a USDA Organic symbol on their produce doesn't mean they're not farming organically. That USDA symbol takes many years and a lot of money to obtain.

Farmers Markets

A farmers market is a group of farmers who sell their products once or twice weekly at a predetermined location (usually a park or other public place). Some farmers markets are very social events, with live music, food vendors and more. Ask around or check the Internet for markets in your community. In addition to inexpensive fresh produce, you'll probably find crafts, homemade goodies, and varieties you've never seen before. Farmers will be happy to give you cooking suggestions and, if you ask nicely, they'll give you samples too.

Everyone wins. In traditional grocery stores, only 18 cents of every dollar you spend goes to the grower. By contrast, growers at farmers markers get to keep up to 90 cents of each dollar you spend on their produce. The payoff for you is that the cost of farmers markets produce compared to conventional grocery produce is on average, 10 to 40% cheaper! *(sustainabletable.org and localharvest.org)*

Nice to know: *58% of farmers markets participate in WIC food coupons, food stamps and local and/or state nutrition programs – helping to make locally grown and sustainable options affordable for all income levels.*

Community Supported Agriculture

Community Supported Agriculture (more commonly known as CSA) is a great way for consumers to work with local farms. You make a financial commitment to the farm, thus becoming a CSA "member" (or "shareholder" or "subscriber") for a growing season, which usually runs from late spring to early fall. Some CSAs will even ask that members contribute a few work hours to the farm during the growing season. It's really up to the CSA to set its rules, and all you have to do is ask what's required. But it's always worth it, no matter what. In exchange for your commitment, you'll reap a regular basket of wonderful, fresh-from-the-earth produce – produce that you helped create! CSAs have increased from just 50 in the U.S. in the 1990s to over 1000 in 2008. (See the Appendix for ways to find farmers' markets and CSAs in your area.)

> ☞ *A typical CSA basket during the growing season runs about $15 to $25 and includes enough fruits and vegetables to feed a family of four for a week. CSA basket portions may vary, so make sure you discuss portion sizes with your local CSA before signing up.*

Food Co-op

A food cooperative is owned by the consumers, the workers or a combination of both. There are usually options you can choose for how you'd like to participate. A food co-op typically supports locally grown produce and is committed to high quality food products, consumer education and input from members for improvements. It's like a grocery store that you get to have an active say in.

U-Pick

Lots of farms open their gates to the public during harvest season to hand-pick their own produce. Going to a U-pick farm is a great family activity or even a nice idea for a date. There is nothing like picking your own strawberries, blueberries or tomatoes on a summer day and eating them right there, on the spot! Kids love it, but usually come home covered in fruit.

Farm Stand

We've all seen those shacks by the side of the highway. They're a fixture in the American landscape. They're also a throwback to a time when all produce was locally produced. Usually they're only open during the harvest season. Sometimes these stands are right next to the same field where the produce was just picked, and sometimes they collect produce from several farms in the area. Either way, it's a good bet you'll get some good, fresh, local food there and may even be able to pick your own.

Right in Your Own Backyard

Maybe the most obvious – and overlooked – option is growing your own garden. While you probably won't be able to meet all your family's produce needs with your backyard garden (but hey, maybe you can!), you can get a lot of other benefits. First of all, you'll be amazed at how much your plants do yield. A single potted tomato plant will keep you in marinara sauce for weeks.

Share some of the bounty with your neighbors or freeze your extras to enjoy off-season. Don't have room for a garden? Many types of produce can be grown in large pots. A porch with some sun is all you need. A window box on a sunny side of the building makes a nice herb garden (rosemary, thyme or oregano) for your salads, even if you live in a city apartment (all you need is a window!). Gardening is one of the most relaxing activities known to humankind. It's easy, and nothing will taste better than the food you grow yourself.

Beyond the Backyard

Love to have a real garden but don't have the room? Think about organizing a community Victory Garden. In World War II millions of people joined together in schoolyards, parks and vacant lots to cultivate Victory Gardens – and helped supply the nation with much needed produce during a time of scarcity. With rising food costs pinching many families' finances, the idea is coming back into style all over the United States as well as in England. It's a nice way to show your commitment to your community, and then sharing the bounty. Is there a spot in your yard, your neighborhood or local park where you could start a Victory Garden? Most communities have vacant plots of land that can be subdivided for small gardens. Families can team with neighbors to divvy up the responsibilities, and everyone benefits. Called **community gardens**, they follow the same principles as the Victory Gardens, and yield the same delicious results.

AND THE WINNER IS...YOU!

Making the move from grocery chains to local sources for your fruits, veggies and other foods can yield savings well into the **hundreds of dollars** every year on your grocery bill. Also, local dairy farms often give discounts to local folks who purchase milk, cheese, butter or meat straight from the farm (but you might want to trade off your pick-up trips with your neighbors, to save time and gas).

SEED MONEY

Cost for an average packet of seeds:

Tomatoes — $2.75
Green beans — $2.49
Strawberries — $2.50
Squash — $1.50
Lettuce — $2.00

Buyer beware: *Unless you have lots of room for the number of plants all those seeds will grow into (you'll be surprised), consider paying a little more ($1.50 to $5.50) for a more mature single plant. An established plant will also give you a jump-start on the season.*

three

The "V" Word

Before you skip this section because you are a bona fide meat-eater, take a second to learn how you can really save money at the grocery store! Eating more vegetarian meals is one of the easiest ways to quickly cut food costs while not skimping on nutrition.

VEGETARIANS (They may be onto something!)

Generally speaking, a vegetarian is someone who doesn't eat meat. Some may also choose to avoid animal by-products, such as dairy and honey. So who are these people and what do they eat?

A Handy Field Guide

There are many types of vegetarians. Here are the most common:

Ovo-lacto vegetarians *do not eat meat (including fish) but will eat eggs, dairy and honey.*

Lacto vegetarians *do not eat meat (including fish) or eggs, but will eat dairy and honey.*

Ovo vegetarians *do not eat meat (including fish) or dairy, but they will eat eggs and honey.*

Vegans *do not eat meat (including fish) or dairy, eggs or honey; many avoid using leather and other animal-based products as well.*

There are other kinds of vegetarians, such as **pescetarians** *(who will eat fish or other seafood),* **pollotarians** *(who will eat poultry), and* **flexitarians** *(specific animals are consumed on rare occasions).*

You may already fit into one of these categories and not even know it!

The practice of avoiding meat products dates back at least as far as the ancient Greeks in the 6th century BC, and perhaps even earlier, to ancient India. The reasons then were as varied as they are now: Cultural taboos or religious doctrines make eating certain animals a no-no, eating meat has some unwanted health consequences, and many people simply don't like the ethical implication of harming animals unnecessarily. And lately, we've learned a lot more about the serious economic and environmental impact of eating animal products vs. choosing a vegetarian option.

Let's look at a few of the reasons you might consider going vegetarian – if even just for a few meals a week.

You will save money. On average, dietary protein from non-animal sources is 30 to 60% cheaper than protein from animal sources (see page 10 for some informative price comparisons).

> ☞ *Real money (for a family of 4): If you simply substitute one tofu or lentils meal in place of one chicken meal each week (that's 1 meal out of 21), at the end of the year you will have saved over $200. If you substitute 5 non-meat meals per week, at the end of the year you will have saved **over $1000**!*

You will improve your health. The American Medical Association has recently recommended the Mediterranean diet as the most successful diet for optimal health. Interestingly, this diet consists mostly of fruits, vegetables, whole grains, beans, lentils and healthy fats – all primary components of a balanced vegetarian diet.

You will <u>really</u> help the environment. A meat-based diet requires nearly seven times the land resources of a plant-based diet: Raising animals for our food supply uses far more energy and water than raising fruits, grains and vegetables; and factory farming produces hundreds of thousands of tons of environmental pollution every year (we're talking manure here, as well as lots of toxic gases and chemicals). Each time you choose to eat vegetarian, you're helping reduce the massive burden of livestock farming on the environment.

Some Talking Points
(for your skeptical friends and family members)

Vegetarians have a lower risk of developing diabetes, heart disease and almost all types of cancer. Ongoing large studies of Seventh Day Adventists (who espouse a vegetarian diet and healthy lifestyle) show this and more, including significantly longer productive years of life.

- If every person in America ate only one cheeseburger a week for an entire year, that's the equivalent of releasing an extra 65,250,000 metric tons of CO_2 per year into the environment. *(openthefuture.com)* And guess how many cheeseburgers the average American actually eats each week – almost three! CO_2, by the way, is a greenhouse gas and one of the most important causes of climate change.

- Eating too much red meat (3 or more servings **per week**) has long been linked to the development of colon cancer, lymph node cancer, prostate cancer and heart disease, to name a few.

Science Fact
Cowabunga! *The average cow produces 75% more methane than any other animal (yes, we mean cow flatulence and manure). With over 1.2 billion cows worldwide, this accounts for nearly 30% of all global methane emissions, another primary culprit in global warming. (epa.gov)*

The Last Word

Eating more vegetarian meals is the single most effective way to save money on your grocery bill. With good planning, you'll still get all the vitamins, minerals and nutrients you and your family need to be healthy. Trust me...and all those millions of healthy, less-meat-eating folks out there!

Creating a great vegetarian meal requires only small changes in your current diet. And you don't even have to mention the "V" word to your die-hard friends or family. Just give them something delicious and hearty to eat and let the good food speak for itself.

Take It To The Bank

10 Best Food Strategies
&
Total Food Dollars Saved

1. **Buy produce in season.** Have you ever seen how much a wintertime basket of berries costs? Ouch. Off-season produce usually requires much more energy and resources to produce and transport, and it often retains less nutritional value too. **Buying in-season produce only can skim $250 or more off your yearly grocery bill.**

2. **If you can't afford fresh, try frozen or canned.** It's usually cheaper to buy frozen or canned fruits and veggies, rather than fresh produce at the chain markets. Nutritionally, fresh is best, but frozen is a close second. Canned is fine too, if price is an issue; just make sure you're always getting organic, and not a lot of added sugar or sodium. **Depending on where you live, if you buy frozen or canned, you can save $200 a year and up on your grocery bill.**

3. **Support your local farmer.** Take advantage of your local farms, farmers markets, co-ops and CSAs. They are cheaper for many reasons and the money you spend stays in your community – maybe even to a farming neighbor! Costs to the consumer are much lower when you buy from local farmers – so you will reap financial and health benefits (as well as supporting your community). **Depending on where you live, you can save $300 a year and up by buying local produce.**

4. **Grow your own garden...and your bank account!** If you have the time and the room, you'll reap huge financial benefits. An average garden can supply a family of four with at least half of your fruit and veggie needs – all for the cost of a few seed packets or small plants, a bit of watering and some TLC. **Conservative estimates for money saved on growing your own produce range from the $750 range...and up.**

5. **Forget processed foods.** This includes not only fast food and eating out, but a lot of the pre-packaged stuff in the grocery. Each individual and family is different

– whether you eat out all the time or hardly ever – so it's tough to say just how much you could save by saying goodbye to processed foods. At least consider ways to bring more whole foods into your diet. **If you substitute one whole-foods meal per week for one processed meal, you will be saving at least $150 a year (multiply this times four for a family of four).**

6. **Try at least one vegetarian meal a week**. You will save money on your weekly grocery bill! And it's easier to cook a delicious vegetarian meal than you might imagine. When you've mastered one veggie meal a week, try to increase to two, and so on. It will add up: **Having just one veggie meal a week can save you $200 a year; five meals a week saves $1000 a year!**

7. **Introduce soy milk to the dairy mix.** If you buy two gallons of cow's milk a week, try substituting soy milk for one of those gallons. **You can save about $3 a gallon and $150 in a year.**

8. **Buy in bulk – organic food only, of course!** In larger wholesale clubs there are some great deals to be found on organic grains, cereals, canned goods, meat or chicken, beans and lentils, and much more. Be sure the packaging is minimal – that helps reduce your consumer impact on the planet while you're saving a few bucks. **Depending on your family's size, you can save $300 and up on properly packaged bulk products.**

9. **Cook in bulk and freeze portions for later use.** Make Saturdays or Sundays cooking days and make several meals or entrees in bulk. Freeze in portion-size containers for easy reheating. Don't have time to cook? Learn to love your crock pot and Dutch oven. Prep time for a crock pot or Dutch oven meal is typically 15 minutes or less, and the end result is a large, home-cooked meal filled with veggies and other good stuff. **We can safely venture to say you'll save at least $300 per year on cooking in bulk.**

10. **Make your own all-purpose flour-based mix.** Look for our basic flour mix recipe at **wecanlivegreen.com**. With slight variations to the basic recipe, it can make delicious breads, pancakes, cakes, and more. And it can be stored for months at a time. This is an old WWII trick that kept a lot of people in the U.S. from missing out on their favorite recipes in food rationing times. **Steering clear of prepackaged mixes can save you $100-plus a year.**

If you implemented just seven out of ten of these food tips and brought them into your life, you could save a minimum of $1,200 a year. And that is a *very* conservative estimate.

Part Two

You and Your Clothes

The Goal: Purchasing clothing that has the smallest negative impact on your health and the environment, while staying within your budgetary constraints. Oh, and it needs to look good too.

The Reality: Most of the clothes we wear are made with fibers that have gone through multiple chemical processes (either toxic, safe or questionable) during their production and creation. In addition, there are ethical considerations, since many of our fabrics and clothing are created and assembled by individuals working in deplorable circumstances (Bangladesh, China, etc.). Not to mention the transportation and energy issues involved in getting the clothes to us.

The Strategy: Knowing the story behind the labels, then finding sources of clothing that line up with your ethical values, your budget, your health concerns and your desire to lighten your environmental footprint. It's not as hard as it sounds.

four

Fashioning A New Look

We all need clothes. We don't need clothes the way we need food, water, air and shelter – but for all intents and purposes, we need clothes. They keep us comfortable, they express our individuality and taste. We spend a lot of time, thought and money on our clothes. But aside from the label, the price and the trendiness of an item, few of us know the story behind the clothes we're wearing. And you might be surprised. It's well worth a bit of sleuthing. Three important questions to ask:

What is it made of?

Where was it made?

How much energy was used to get it to me?

What is It Made Of?

Over 97% of clothes items are made from the following two materials: cotton (40%) and synthetic fibers (57%). Let's look first at cotton:

Cotton is the most common natural fiber in use today (other natural or animal fibers include wool, silk, hemp and bamboo). Total international trade of cotton is over 12 billion dollars yearly. In many developing countries hungry for economic growth, cotton is referred to as "white gold."

Traditionally grown cotton – It seems logical to assume that cotton is nice and natural. And it is, but… Traditionally grown cotton is cultivated with a heavy use of pesticides and insecticides. In fact, cotton makes up 11% of total global pesticide use and 25% of total global insecticide use, which is an astounding number for one single agricultural group.

So we need to be aware of chemicals in the fabrics we use, just as we are with our foods. The chemicals that are used to control pests and insects on crops (including cotton) soak into the ground, water supply, into the air and into the environment as a whole – which eventually affects all living things on the planet. The flip side of this picture is that not all cotton is grown this way.

Organic cotton – Just as there are organic foods, there is organic cotton, grown without pesticides or other man-made chemicals. If you have young children or elderly family members, you might want to help lessen their exposure to these chemicals by switching them over to organic cotton – starting with sheets and night clothes, which have the most contact with their bodies. **Nice to know:** Wal-Mart, Target and Bed Bath & Beyond have 100% organic cotton twin sheet sets for under $30. And Baby-Wise.com sells 100% organic cotton crib sheets for $10.95.

Synthetic (man-made) fibers – Synthetics are in 57% of our clothing, and they're created in a number of different ways: Nylon comes entirely from petrochemicals (materials made from petroleum or hydrocarbons). Acrylic, polyester, acetate and olefin all undergo a series of chemical processes in order to be made into clothing. Rayon (not considered a true synthetic because it's made from a cellulose material) also goes through several chemical processes before it's finally usable as a clothing textile. I'm not saying that these are necessarily harmful, but the closer you stay to simple and natural and away from highly processed products, the better it is all around – and the smaller the environmental footprint.

Knowing the Toxins

The EPA establishes tolerance limits to pesticides or MRLs (maximum residue levels) that establish how much pesticide residue is tolerated for our food and product supply. Tolerance limits have been established for imported and domestic products. Some pesticides are exempted from a tolerance limit.

Take a good look at your closet. It may seem strange that clothing can come into contact with pesticides, insecticides or chemicals of any kind, but the following are the most common places where your clothing item may have been in contact with chemicals or harmful substances:

- **In the creation of the raw materials** of the clothing (traditionally grown cotton and the use of pesticides/insecticides, synthetic fibers and the chemical processes used to create the fiber)

- **In the production of the raw materials** to create the final product (synthetic fiber chemical processes, dyeing processes, chemicals added to create or alter the natural or synthetic fiber)

It is hard to know just how many chemicals we can be exposed to without harm to our bodies. We Can Live Green goes by the common sense method: Because all living things have the same operating system of DNA (deoxyribonucleic acid) that exists in different combinations based upon the organism, it makes sense to think that if a substance is harmful to one organism it just might be harmful to other organisms that come into contact with the substance as well. (See the Appendix for some Simple Science info.)

Now, we realize the story is a bit more complicated than this, but we think this is an important first step in taking a bit more critical view of the substances around us and how these substances might affect our bodies. We might not have all the answers at the moment, but the answers we do have point overwhelmingly to the direction of "The fewer toxic chemicals in our bodies, the better."

Many scientists would argue that toxic chemicals have replaced bacteria and viruses as the greatest threat to human health. A study in Minnesota found significantly higher rates of birth defects in children whose parents are pesticide applicators.

☞ *Here a phrase you'll be hearing a lot in the coming days: "company transparency." This means that a company reveals its positive and negative impacts on the planet through its manufacturing, distribution and production efforts to consumers. The outdoor clothing manufacturer Patagonia is a prime example of company transparency.*

Where is It Made?

There are arguments on both sides about importing clothing and textiles. We won't get into the whole importing debate – rather, we'd like you to think about a few things as you make your next clothing purchases. And yes, we know that clothing is usually cheaper when it's made in 3rd world countries, and none of us wants to spend money unnecessarily. It's not easy to turn away from a bargain price, especially in a tough economy. But...

The top 5 countries that exported <u>finished clothing</u> to the United States in 2005 (over 80 billion dollars)

China
Mexico
India
Indonesia
Bangladesh

The top 5 countries that exported <u>textiles</u> to the United States in 2005 (over 22 billion dollars)

> China
> Canada
> India
> South Korea
> Mexico

If you look on the label of a clothing item and see it was made in another country, you might ask yourself, Under what conditions was this made? How was the material grown and harvested? Just who exactly made this item…a child, a forced laborer? How was this person compensated for their work? If you'd like to know the back story of your apparel, we suggest contacting your favorite clothing labels to find out more. Again, the answers might surprise you. And you might also be surprised at what companies out there are making their practices known to consumers so that consumers can make a well-informed decision on their next purchases. Banana Republic, for one. And on the more pricey end of women's wear, the Eileen Fisher line.

How Much Energy Was Used to Get It to Me?

Few of us know much about the amount of energy used to create the clothing item and then get it to us. Company transparency on energy used to create a product (and the product's subsequent carbon footprint) is a new and rapidly growing trend. In 2008 in England, companies began to implement a carbon footprint index on food items – allowing buyers to put an environmental impact number on items they are considering purchasing.

In the United States, maverick clothing company Patagonia has created a website, called The Footprint Chronicles, which gives consumers the inside scoop on select Patagonia products – showing the footprints these products are leaving behind.

What are My Options? (and we're not suggesting clothing optional!)

Our organization, We Can Live Green, is a big fan of "less is more" – maybe you don't really, really need that new shirt as badly as you think! However, if you can't live without it, do a little investigating. What's the story behind what you are wearing? What is it made of? Where is it made? How much energy was used to get it to you? The more people who ask these questions, the quicker we'll see a change in the market-place. And the more options will be made available to you.

Carbon footprint:

The combined effect of all that we humans, individually and collectively, are doing that causes elevated levels of carbon dioxide, which in turn increases the "greenhouse effect" and hastens global warming. You have a measurable footprint and so does your car and your house and the clothes on your back.

Now, because this book promises that your new green knowledge can translate into money in your pocket, it's time to tell you how. Let's take it to the bank!

Take It To The Bank

8 Best Clothing Strategies
&
Total Apparel Dollars Saved

1. **Frequent the resale, thrift and vintage shops.** The selections are amazing! And you can save a lot of money. These shopping trips can be fun for the whole family – the great thing about a resale shop is you never know what you might find. It's an adventure for everyone! Depending on your typical clothing budget, buying items at half to two-thirds below the price of a department store can add up fast. **We can safely estimate a minimun savings of $400 per year.**

2. **Embrace hand-me-downs – from friends, family members and fashionable neighbors.** Participate in giving hand-me-downs too! Be creative – organize a "swap till you drop" party. There are lots of ways to save money and share your clothing with others, all while getting a few new duds of your own. An especially good option if you have children, since they often outgrow their clothing before our pocketbooks are ready for another trip to the store. **Depending on your usual clothing expenses, you can save $200 to $400 a year and more.**

3. **Look for sweatshop-free, fair trade and organic clothing options.** There are tons of great-looking options out there! Get on the Internet and type in some of those key words. You'll be delighted at what pops up.

4. **Spend more on less.** Sound like a contradictory statement? If you focus on purchasing ethical, high-quality products, the product will last longer due to superior construction and design and you will sleep at night worry-free, knowing you're voting your conscience with your dollar.

5. **Spend the money to resole shoes and repair tattered clothing.** You can either do this yourself (maybe not the resoling your shoes part) or pay someone to do this

(almost every community has a local cobbler who is gifted at springing new life into a sad pair of shoes). **Doing this, you can safely save at least $100 per year.**

6.   **Focus your more expensive purchases on wardrobe basics** – clothing staples in styles that transcend fads. That's what our mothers and grandmothers always did, before we became such a fast-change, throwaway consumer culture. But we can move beyond that wasteful pattern. Today, it's all about being smart and savvy with the basics.

7.   **For trendier accents in your wardrobe, go big on accessories** like jewelry, scarves, shoes and bags.

8.   **Dust off the old sewing machine.** We know you may not have the time to make your own apparel or your children's, but the ultimate money-saver will always be in the things you create yourself. Just be sure to ask the right questions about your fabrics at the fabric shop! Nothing gets more personal style points than creating your own apparel! **You can easily save $250-plus per year by making some of your own clothes.**

If you implemented even a small part of the clothing options that we've put a dollar value to here, you can anticipate saving at least $500-plus a year. This is a low-end estimate, just to be sure we're not promising more than is realistic. But it's a no-brainer that you'll come out way ahead!

Part Three

You And Your Car
(Transportation in an Age of Limits)

The Goal: Getting where you need to go as cheaply, comfortably, safely and efficiently as possible, while keeping in mind your transportation impact on the environment and your health.

The Reality: Rapidly increasing transportation costs have put a strain on every budget. But if buying a new vehicle is out of the question right now, and you're stuck with the gas guzzler you have, you could use some help making the most of what you've got — and knowing how to plan for your next purchase.

The Strategy: Understanding how transportation fits into the going-green picture, and what alternatives are available to you right now as a consumer: how to save on fuel costs, how to minimize your car's impact on the environment, and what transportation alternatives are out there for you. Employing short- and long-term goals to lessen your transportation's negative impact on your pocketbook, health and the planet.

five

Getting Where You Need To Go

A set of wheels and personal freedom are synonymous images in American culture. We learn to love our "wheels" at an early age. Whether it's a pair of roller skates, a skateboard or a bike as a child, or our city transportation system or the oh-so-memorable first vehicle as a teenager – we have all learned to love the ability to get where we need to go. And who can blame us? A set of wheels not only represents individual freedom, it represents good times, the promise of adventure.

So, the fact that we now hear that our adult wheels are playing a major role in the pain we feel in our wallets, as well as harming the environment, well...it's downright upsetting. Our cars are our links to our independence. And our jobs. And now you tell me I'm destroying the planet because of the type of car I drive? Can my car's carbon footprint really be that big?

Sorry, but the bad news is **Yes**. The good news is, there are no carbon footprint police coming to get you. But that is also bad news, because that means you can ignore – for just a while longer – the fact that your car is the single largest contributing factor to your carbon footprint.

Some average U.S. carbon footprints per person:
- Driving and Flying 44.3%
- Home Energy 36.2%
- Food and Diet 15.1%
- Recycling and Waste 4.4%

(Nature Conservancy)

Record-setting increases in gasoline prices are forcing most of us to reevaluate our current transportation options. This affects every aspect of our lives, from transportation to food to any other consumer good we buy. Because of the huge strain on our pocketbooks, we are all looking for answers – now!

When there's no more oil – One way or another, we're going to have to change the way we get around, simply because oil is a non-renewable resource. Once there's no oil left, there is really *no more oil*. Some reports state that the global oil supply will peak in the coming decades, others argue that peak oil occurred in 2005. Regardless, no one thinks the price of oil is going down very much any time soon, if ever. Even if we had a never-ending supply of oil on the planet, global demand has increased significantly due to industrialization of developing countries.

What can we do? The best strategies for your budget, your health and, yes, the planet, will involve two things: **Short-term strategies** (increasing your fuel efficiency, and other quick fixes for your transportation budget). That's what this chapter is all about: what you can do right now to give yourself some relief. And **Long-term strategies** (exploring your options and planning for your next vehicle). The next chapter will analyze the fuels available today and the ones that are on the horizon, to help you prepare for your next purchase.

SHORT-TERM STRATEGIES
(While Keeping Your Present Car)

The tricky thing about purchasing a new, greener vehicle is that while it can greatly benefit your pocketbook in the long run (and the environment immediately), many of us simply do not have the available cash to make the big change right now. So, if you're stuck with the vehicle you're driving today, how can you save on fuel costs and help it run as efficiently as possible?

Finding The Cheapest Gas

- *Plan to fill up your tank on a midweek morning. Most gas stations increase their rates for the weekend and prices typically stabilize by midweek.*

- *Consider joining a wholesale club – gas is usually cheaper here. However, you will have to pay a membership fee, so do the math before you commit a membership to the club.*

- *Gas stations in wealthier neighborhoods, with auto repair shops or car washes, and next to major highways typically have more expensive gasoline.*

- *Before starting a road trip, consider comparing gas prices county-by-county and state-by-state to find the best deals. Plan your pit stops accordingly.*

- *Learn to use (and love) websites such as GasPriceWatch.com and gasbuddy.com to check out the cheapest gas stations in your area and across the country.*

- *Fill up three days before a holiday to avoid holiday price increases.*

Organize your car excursions. (You may already be doing this already, but just in case...) Bundle your errands. Grocery, cleaners, dog groomer. Going way across town? See if you can do several longer errands on one specific day of the week. [🌴 – 🌴🌴 and FREE]

Start a school/work carpool. Offer to give kids/coworkers in the neighborhood rides to school/work and split the cost. Or alternate days with other parents/coworkers in the neighborhood so that everyone shares the responsibility and the savings. Check out RideSearch.com, NuRide.com and eRideShare.com, for carpools in your neighborhood. [🌴🌴 and FREE – $$]

Negotiate an "off-peak hours" work schedule with your employer. You'll save gas and carbon emissions by not idling so long in congested traffic. [🌴🌴 and FREE]

Say goodbye to the 2 to 4 car family habit. It may create a few more minutes of coordination among housemates, but getting rid of even one of your household vehicles stacks up to big savings. [🌴🌴🌴 and FREE]

> **Fun fact:**
> Watch the wholesale unleaded futures prices – when they're on the rise, you can be sure that the price at the pump will soon go up!

Get a credit card with gas rebates. [🏃 and FREE]

Treat your car like the finely-tuned machine that it is. This will add up to much better gas mileage for you and it will help the environment (a poorly maintained car can release as much as 10 times more emissions than a car that is well maintained and in good working condition). *(www.nsc.org)* [🏃 – 🏃🏃 and FREE – $$]

---

10 Mileage Boosters

1. *Don't drive with a heavy foot – obey the speed limits! And cut out the quick stops and starts from lights and stop signs.*

2. *Check and maintain appropriate tire pressure. Use tire recommendations on the tire wall, not the doorframe or fuel filler flap.*

3. *Use tires with good tread. "Low resistance tires" are reported to be the best for gas mileage.*

4. *Check and change the air filter often. Consider spending a bit extra for a more efficient filter.*

5. *Perform regular maintenance – including oil changes every 3,000 miles and tune-ups twice a year.*

6. *Use cruise control and overdrive to assist in maximizing mileage.*

7. *Use the right octane – it's essential for proper engine function.*

8. *Use the A/C sparingly. Doing errands around town? Consider rolling down the windows. Drag created by rolled down windows should not be an issue for in-town driving.*

9. *Check and maintain your braking system – a poorly functioning brake system negatively affects mileage.*

10. *Remove unnecessary weight in your car, like ski and luggage racks – the more weight (and drag), the more gas you will use.*

Go electric! – If you live in a suburb where errands, schools and other commitments are close to your home (and in 45 mph zones or lower), consider an electric vehicle – with zero emissions, no gasoline costs (ever!). Costing about $12,000, there are several great models out there and some really exciting options coming in 2009 and 2010 that reach highway speeds of 60 mph-plus! [🏃🏃🏃 and $$$]

Try a motorized bike. Drive a small motorcycle or scooter and pay less at the pump, and pay less often! But be aware that motorcycles are heavy polluters (10 times more polluting per mile than a passenger vehicle, according to the California Air Resources Board). As an alternative, check out some of the nifty electric bicycles out there. [🌴🌴 and $$ – $$$]

Myths & Facts

Myth: It takes more gasoline to turn the car on and off than to idle.

Fact: Idling for longer than 20 seconds uses more fuel (and creates more pollution) than simply restarting the car.

Myth: Idling the car doesn't burn a significant amount of gas.

Fact: Every 15 minutes of idling burns a quarter of a gallon of gasoline (that's dollars worth of gasoline we're talking about here!).

Myth: The car has to "warm up" before I drive it.

Fact: Most cars are now computer-controlled with fuel-injected engines. Manufacturers claim that these engines warm up **within 30 seconds** – so no "warm-up" period is necessary.

Shift gears! Consider a manual transmission, which typically gets better mileage than an automatic. Manual transmission is usually cheaper too, so you save money twice! Also, with a manual you can coast to stoplights in neutral and save gas. [🌴 – 🌴🌴]

2 Useful Gadgets

An OBDII reader device – This will provide you with real-time information on your mileage and fuel efficiency. The cost: $150 to $350, depending on the brand (such as ScanGauge or Equus 3130) and cables needed. [🌴 and $$]

GPS – A global positioning system can help you navigate through traffic and find the shortest route to anywhere you are traveling. Saves gas, time and temper. The cost: $250 to $699, depending on the brand (such as Garmin's Nuvi or Magellan's Maestro) [🌴 and $$]

Use your mass transit systems. Think you can't make a difference? One person using mass transit for a year, instead of driving to work, will keep 9.1 pounds of hydrocarbons, 62.5 pounds of carbon monoxide, and 4.9 pounds of nitrogen oxides **out of the air we all breathe.** *(www.nsc.org)* [🚶🚶🚶 and $]

And the obvious conclusion: If you want to save money on gasoline and help the planet, don't drive! You can walk, ride a scooter or skateboard or bike, use mass transit...it's your call! [🚶🚶🚶 and FREE]

Facts & Figures For Your Consideration

- **Ridesharing stat:** By ridesharing to work every day, The National Safety Council calculates that you can save over **$3,000 a year** on gas, insurance, parking, and wear and tear on your car. Also, if a commuter designates an automobile for pleasure use only, the insurance premiums on that car can go down as much as **20 percent.** *(www.nsc.org)*

- **AAA** estimates the cost of operating a car at roughly **70 cents** per mile – and going up!

- **Follow that UPS truck!** UPS has figured out how to decrease fuel costs and their carbon footprint. In 2007, by simply programming more right turns than left turns into their routes, UPS cut **30 million miles** off its deliveries, saved **3 million gallons of gas**, while lowering CO_2 emissions by **32,000 metric tons**...equal to the emissions of 5300 passenger cars. The moral? Small changes in everyday habits can reap big financial benefits and help the environment!

- **Three harmful chemicals your car releases:** <u>Hydrocarbons</u> (cause eye irritation, coughing, shortness of breath and leads to permanent lung damage); <u>Nitrogen Oxides</u> (contribute to the formation of ozone and contribute to acid rain and water quality issues); <u>Carbon monoxide</u> (a deadly gas that reduces the flow of oxygen to the brain and can impair mental functioning). Motor vehicles in our cities are responsible for up to 90% of carbon monoxide in the atmosphere. *(www.nsc.org)*

Preparing for the Long-term

We're looking ahead to the coming developments in fuels, as well as the vehicles they will power. Change is in the air. It's an exciting time, between a past that didn't serve us well and future transportation options that we hope will be kinder to our planet, our health and our pocketbooks.

The next chapter is all about fuels, including gasoline: what's good, what's not so good, what's available now and what's on the horizon. And some strategies for the years ahead.

six

All About Fuels

a quick-reference guide

This chapter provides you with a comparison rundown of the seven primary types of fuel that are used in our vehicles today, or that are being developed for general use in the near future. Here, you will find a brief profile of the seven fuels, how they work, the pros and cons of each, the costs, fuel efficiency and – perhaps most important – their carbon emissions. I hope that this information will help guide your planning for your next vehicle purchase. **Note:** Under "Cost" you'll find that sometimes a fuel's cost is given and at other times an alternative *vehicle's* cost is given instead. It should become apparent why that is.

Gasoline

Availability: Gasoline engines are the most widely used mechanized transportation mode across the globe.

How it works: Gasoline engines utilize high-energy fuel (gasoline) run through a small, enclosed space. The combustion of the air/fuel mixture creates energy that propels the vehicle.

Pros: Gasoline engines are readily accessible everywhere and come in a variety of prices, sizes and uses.

Cons: With rising gasoline costs and climate change an increasing issue, gasoline engines no longer seem to be the best alternative for many of us.

Cost: The cost of running a vehicle on gasoline varies widely, depending on age, make and model.

Fuel efficiency: Average fuel efficiency for an average sedan is 23 mpg – more for an economy car, and less for an SUV or truck.

Carbon emissions: Gasoline engines produce significant carbon emissions, the leading cause of climate change – approximately 19.4 pounds of CO_2 per gallon for the average vehicle.

Diesel

Availability: Diesel engines are sold by practically every automaker, and they service a variety of lifestyles. After a bit of a hiatus from American culture, diesel vehicles are making a resurgence in 2008 and 2009, due to their improved emissions ratings (look for clean-burning diesel engines) and significantly better gas mileage.

How it works: Diesel engines use chemical energy to power mechanical energy in the form of the movement of pistons. Energy is released through small explosions as the fuel is compressed. These explosions propel the car forward.

Pros: Diesel emits smaller amounts of carbon monoxide, hydrocarbons and other gases than gasoline engines – and gets significantly better mileage than gasoline engines. Recent improvements have also reduced smog emissions. Most exciting of all, a diesel engine is able to run on **biodiesel** – a non-petroleum-based oil made from plant material or animal fat – with little or no modifications. If converted, diesel engines are also able to run on vegetable oil and other plant sources. These options are significantly better for your pocketbook *and* the environment!

Cons: On a per-gallon comparison, an older, straight diesel engine running on diesel emits a slightly higher amount of CO_2 into the atmosphere than a gasoline engine. Due to recent industrial development and global demand, diesel now costs more per gallon than gasoline. Older diesel engines emit higher concentrations of nitrogen compounds as well as particulate matter, which lead to poor health conditions, acid rain and smog. Check out statistics on the newer, clean burning diesel engines for their nitrogen and particulate matter emissions. Running your car on biodiesel or other plant products produces very low emissions, and the fuel is 1/3 to 1/2 the cost of gasoline or diesel (but these alternative fuels can be hard to come by, depending on where you live).

Cost: The cost of a diesel vehicle varies. They are typically slightly more expensive than a gasoline-powered vehicle. Most argue the cost is offset by the fuel alternatives available for use in diesel engines – which necessitate a conversion kit (see Footnote).*

---

*Conversion kits are available in select cities and on the Internet to convert your diesel engine to run on **straight vegetable oil or waste vegetable oil**. While regulations vary from state to state and are in the process of being modified in many states, vegetable oil offers a cheap alternative to diesel fuels. Check your state regulations on vegetable oil as fuel before committing your car to a conversion.

Fuel efficiency: Diesel engines have a higher energy density than gasoline, which is why they typically have higher fuel efficiency than a standard gasoline engine. Diesel engines may get as much as 15 to 30-plus more miles per gallon than their gasoline counterparts.

Carbon emissions: Older diesel engines produce approximately 22.2 pounds per gallon of CO_2, which is more than a gasoline engine. Newer engines typically run cleaner.

Biodiesel

Availability: Biodiesel is just emerging as a fuel alternative to gasoline and diesel; therefore, availability differs regionally.

How it works: Biodiesel works with little or no modification in diesel engines. Biodiesel is a plant-based or animal fat-based oil. Biodiesel vehicles can run on diesel, or a mixture of diesel and biodiesel, or on straight biodiesel. There are different grades of biodiesel, ranging from B5 to B100, and availability varies from region to region.

Pros: Biodiesel has lower CO_2 emissions than gasoline or diesel engines. Using biodiesel reduces dependency on foreign oils. Biodiesel lubricates the engine, decreasing engine wear. It requires little or no modification to any existing diesel engine.

Cons: Current biodiesel technology causes an increase in nitrogen oxides, which are responsible for smog formation. Biodiesel acts as a solvent which can loosen particles in the engine and clog fuel filters, etc., and there is a slight decrease in fuel economy with biodiesel. And it is not always available. The most significant concern and criticism of biodiesel is the use of agricultural land and clearing of virgin forest to create farmland for this fuel source. **Buyer beware:** You may void your warranty if you run biodiesel in your vehicle. Check with the manufacturer.

Cost: Biodiesel can be used in a diesel engine and costs up to $3.00 per gallon (as of this writing). Some consumers have made agreements with restaurants to take their used vegetable oil off their hands, so you might get your fuel...for free!

Fuel efficiency: Fuel efficiency is the same as, or slightly higher than, that of the diesel engine.

Carbon emissions: Biodiesel carbon emissions are as much as 78.5% lower than that of a gasoline or diesel engine.

Ethanol

Availability: In the U.S., ethanol is very rare, but it is widely used in some other countries, notably, Brazil.

How it works: Ethanol is an alcohol, and highly flammable, but it can combine with gasoline in varying quantities. Most gasoline cars in the U.S. today can run on blends of ethanol and gasoline with up to a 10% ethanol ratio.

Pros: Ethanol can be mass-produced by the fermentation of sugar or corn. It can also be combined with gasoline, which is readily available across the globe. FlexFuel vehicles can run on ethanol (known as E85).

Cons: Ethanol uses a tremendous amount of agricultural land to produce the end product, so we should factor in the energy consumption involved in its production, and the pollution created to bring it to you. Also, as the U.S. and other countries increase the cultivation of corn and other food crops for ethanol, diverting them from food use, experts theorize that widespread famines could be on the horizon.

Cost: Ethanol is about a dollar cheaper than gasoline.

Fuel efficiency: Ethanol is about 30% less efficient than gasoline.

Carbon emissions: Carbon dioxide emissions are 20% less than a typical gasoline powered vehicle.

Hybrid

Availability: Many automakers have at least one hybrid option available for sale in 2008 with more options on the way for 2009 and 2010.

How it works: A hybrid is a combination gasoline engine and electric engine. How the two engines interact depends on the type of hybrid (a parallel hybrid or a series hybrid, for example). The gasoline engine is smaller and more efficient than a conventional gasoline engine. In addition, the hybrid engine stores energy in the battery and shuts off the gasoline engine at times to conserve energy and increase fuel efficiency.

Pros: Hybrids produce between 80 to 95% fewer emissions than a gasoline engine, depending on the vehicle. Hybrids also get 15 to 30-plus **more** miles per gallon than their gasoline engine counterparts. In 2007, sales of hybrids increased 70% for some models, and since then dealers can barely keep up with the general public's increasing enthusiasm – so according to the law of supply and demand, hybrids should become increasingly affordable.

Cons: Drivers accustomed to a certain amount of "get up and go" from their vehicle may experience a slight decrease in power, based on the mechanics of hybrid function. Hybrids are currently more expensive than their gasoline or diesel engine cousins – sometimes by as much as $10,000-plus. Those wishing to stop buying gas at the pump will have to look further than a hybrid – you still have to pay for gas, just less often. Controversy abounds in certain circles as to the total footprint of a hybrid versus a gasoline-powered vehicle, so do your research before picking a side.

Cost: In 2008, hybrids ranged from $21,000 to $56,000, depending on make and model.

Fuel efficiency: The average fuel efficiency depends on the model, but can be estimated at 35 to 40 mpg, with some vehicles reaching as high as 60 mpg.

Carbon emissions: Hybrids emit up to 95% less greenhouse gases into the atmosphere than more traditional counterparts.

Electric

Availability: Limited availability in specific regions in 2008, with more massive scale production in 2009 and 2010.

How it works: The vehicle is propelled forward through an electric drive motor, which obtains electricity through batteries, fuel cells or a generator.

Pros: There are virtually no emissions associated with this vehicle as well as no fuel costs. You can be completely gasoline-independent – which will save you anywhere from $200 and up a month on your monthly bills!

Cons: Battery life, capacity, charging requirements and cost remain an issue for these vehicles. If you travel more than 50 miles per day, current batteries do not stay charged long enough to support your commute. There is also concern for the life of the batteries, and the effect of subsequent battery purchases on the pocketbook.

Cost: To convert a gasoline-powered vehicle to electric, expect to pay up to $10,000 for an electric car conversion kit, not including labor and batteries. Neighborhood Electric Vehicles (NEV) are very affordable ($12,000) but do not exceed 40 mph in most cases. NEVs are very compact, so if you live in a fast-paced, highly trafficked part of the country, consider safety before making this purchase. Other options on the market include high-end sports cars in the $100,000 range. Electric car manufacturers are expected to roll out commuter cars, SUVs and more (all exceeding 65 mph) in the $30,000 range starting in 2009.

Fuel efficiency: You don't have to fuel up, so your fuel efficiency in an electric vehicle is as good as it gets – you simply never have to worry about fuel! You *do* have to worry about keeping your battery charged!

Carbon emissions: Electric vehicles are close to **97% cleaner** than gasoline powered vehicles.

Hydrogen

Availability: Extremely limited availability nationwide with fueling stations currently in a handful of cities.

How it works: Now we're talking about fuel cells, not combustion engines. A fuel cell is an **energy conversion** device in which (in this case) hydrogen reacts with oxygen, producing electricity, which in turn powers the motor.

Pros: Hydrogen cars are completely **emissions-free** – except for water vapor.

Cons: Hydrogen is an energy *carrier*, not an energy *source*, which means refueling is necessary. With just a few fueling stations currently available nationwide, creating the infrastructure to make hydrogen a reality is a long-term and very expensive endeavor (estimated to be at least 10 years to implement). While an exciting new alternative to fossil fuels, the infrastructure does not yet exist to support this fuel source on a massive scale.

Cost: Prices are not yet available for these vehicles, which are found only in select areas as leases and special orders.

Fuel efficiency: Reports are too varied at this point to give an accurate estimate.

Carbon emissions: None. There are no carbon emissions with hydrogen vehicles. The only emission with a hydrogen vehicle is water vapor.

Take It To The Bank

7 Best Transportation Strategies
&
Total Transportation Dollars Saved

1. **Rideshare.** The National Safety Council projects a $3000 yearly saving for commuters who rideshare. I want to be as conservative as possible in my promises, so I can assure you of savings above $2,000 a year, and hope you'll be pleasantly surprised by how much more you will actually save! Anyone out there who can use an extra $2,000 or more right now? Coordinate a commuting strategy with coworkers or neighbors and start saving now: **at least $2,000 a year.**

2. **Use mass transit.** The average bus/train/subway pass for a month ranges from $12 to $85. Compare that against the minimum of $250 spent on gasoline plus insurance costs and car payments for most of us every month. **Monthly savings: at least $175. Yearly savings: $2100 (based on a $75 per month mass transit pass and a low estimate of $250 for car-related costs). And these are minimum estimates of savings!**

3. **Drive less.** If you can't use a rideshare program or mass transit, find ways to drive less. Consider purchasing a motorbike, scooter, bike, skateboard, motorized bike, Segway – or walking. Cost: everything from FREE to $6,000 and up. But you will quickly recuperate your costs by spending less on gasoline. **Either immediately, or within the first several years of owning your alternative wheels, you will have saved at least $2,000.**

4. **Eliminate one family vehicle.** If you can do this, it will save up to $300 a month on gasoline and insurance costs (not even counting car payments). **Minimum cost savings per year to eliminate one vehicle in a household: about $3,600.**

5. **Consider negotiating an "off-peak" schedule at work.** By eliminating the time you spend idling in traffic, you can reduce your gasoline consumption (more money in your pocketbook), improve your health (less stress on your commute) and help out

the planet (less vehicle emissions for our polluted air). **Commute distances vary, but we estimate a conservative savings per year of $350.** It's worth doing your own calculations because this would be great information to share with your employer when negotiating an off-peak schedule!

6. **Designate one car on your car insurance as "for pleasure use only"** – and see your insurance drop by 20%. Just another perk to ridesharing! **Depending on your insurance plan, this can save you hundreds of dollars a year.**

7. **Make your next vehicle purchase count for your pocketbook and the planet.** When you make the switch from gasoline-powered to hybrid, electric, biodiesel or hydrogen, over a five-to-ten-year period you will reap enormous savings: **multiple thousands of dollars.**

Part Four

Family Living
(Secrets of a Toxin-free, Energy-efficient Home)

The Goal: Maintaining a living space with as little exposure to toxic chemicals as possible. Staying within the family budget while helping to improve your health and the environment.

The Reality: Toxic chemicals are in many places in our home, from furniture to personal care items to cleaning products. Little research has been done to fully understand how our exposure to these chemicals affects our health, but the prognosis isn't good.

The Strategy: Knowing the enemy. Informing yourself, friends and family about the toxins at home. Creating a financially feasible short-term and long-term plan to address these issues.

seven

The Down 'N Dirty On Toxins

why you need to know

"There's no place like home." Dorothy was right. No matter what or where you call home, there really is no place quite like it. Studies show we spend an average of 15.6 hours of our day there – even more, if we work from home – so we'd better be sure our time there is helping, not hurting, us!

> **Toxin:** *A poisonous substance; any substance that causes injury, illness or death*

In the natural world there are many toxins, all with a specific purpose – the venom of a rattlesnake or a poison arrow frog, for example. These organisms use their toxins to kill their prey or harm a predator, which helps them stay alive. They also have built-in warning systems (the rattle on a rattlesnake or the bright colors of a poison arrow frog) that warn other organisms that they are armed and dangerous. Fair enough. So, what about toxins made and used by humans? What's their purpose, and what are the warning systems, so I know to stay clear?

Man-made Toxins

Today, most of the poisons on the planet don't come from nature, they come from man. We have created chemicals for all sorts of uses in all sorts of products – from motor oil to batteries to hair dyes to computers to pesticides to plastics to nail polish – all of which have toxic components. When we use these products, dispose of them or do anything else with them, we are releasing these toxic chemicals into our air, our water supply and our environment as a whole. In the United States we have created warning systems for the most toxic of chemicals, labeling products with symbols that represent *Danger*, *Poison* or *Caution*.

Many would argue that we don't have adequate labels for all the toxic chemicals in use today. The truth is, there are well over 100,000 different man-made chemicals floating around on our planet, and we've only tested a small percentage of them to find out their full effect on human health. So, we're not really sure just *how* "toxic" toxic chemicals are to us. In this case, ignorance is definitely not bliss!

How Toxic is Toxic?

Some things may not hurt us if taken in small doses, but too much all at once can be deadly – even aspirin or Tylenol. The word for this is **acute toxicity**, meaning the toxin has a drastic effect on an organism (like death) over a short period of time.

What is far less simple to get a handle on is **chronic toxicity**, the harmful health effects resulting from exposure to a toxin at *low levels* over a period of time. How much of a toxin can a person be exposed to and still be o.k.? What is the line between harmful and harmless over days, years or a life span? Now the picture starts to get fuzzy. And because it's tough to give adequate answers, the "shadow of a doubt" is often raised by the industries that produce them, to defend the use of these chemicals and to downplay people's concerns. So, how can we know for sure if a chemical is dangerous if we can't even adequately test the chemicals? Animal studies are controversial and don't always translate to humans very well, and humans can't be used in such a study (we know we won't be signing up for that study any time soon!).

Our best option is to rely on data from job exposures to chemicals that result in disease. Typically, workers who work around a certain chemical are significantly more likely to develop specific diseases than the general population. For example:

☞ *PVC*
> *A study from the 1980s showed that Swedish workers employed in PVC plants had a significantly higher incidence of liver cancer (up to 3,000 times more) than the general population. PVC, polyvinyl chloride, is a common chemical compound, a plastic used in a wide variety of manufactured products, from garden hoses and rainwear to car upholstery and children's toys.*

Cancer Rates and the Environment

While it's still hard to prove beyond a shadow of a doubt that man-made chemicals cause disease, consider the following: The World Health Organization has estimated that cancer diagnoses will increase from present levels by 50% in 2020, with 15 million new cases estimated in the year 2020 alone.

- *The International Agency for Research on Cancer has concluded that 80% of all cancers can be attributed to environmental influences (this includes lifestyle choices and exposure to toxic chemicals).*

- *One-half of the world's cancers occur among people who live in industrialized countries, even though they are only one-fifth of the world's population.*

- *During our lifetime, 40% of all Americans will get some form of cancer – half of all men and one-third of all women.*

- *Only 5 to 10% of cancers are caused by defective genes – the other 90 to 95% are the result of what we encounter in our environment.*

(Statistics excerpted from Sandra Steingraber's book, "Living Downstream" and the World Health Organization's "World Cancer Report, 2003")

While we wait for scientific certainty about the dangers of toxic chemicals to the human body, we can reasonably assume that widespread use of man-made chemicals must have some type of negative effect on our health and the planet.

eight

The Common Toxins In Your Home

what to do: action items and money-saving tips

Toxins are all around us, but let's focus on what we can immediately begin to change – toxins in the home. What are these toxic chemicals? Where are they located? How do we start getting rid of them? Here are ten of the most common toxic chemicals that could be in your home – and what to do about them.

Asbestos

The issue: Many homes built prior to 1986 still contain asbestos in ductwork, siding, flooring, wrapping for pipes and ceiling material.

What to do: If you think your family may be exposed to asbestos, contact a local asbestos testing professional. Fair warning: Testing can cost several hundred dollars. If you are a renter, request that your landlord arrange for testing.

Lead

The issue: If your home or apartment was built before 1978, when lead-based paints and lead water pipes were the norm, you may still have significant amounts of toxic lead in your environment. Children are most commonly exposed to lead through contact with chipping or peeling paint.

What to do: Hire a professional to test your home for lead – make sure you select a state-certified technician. If your state doesn't certify technicians, look for technicians who have passed EPA guidelines. If you're a renter, your landlord should cover this expense. There are lead testing kits available for $20 to $50, but it's best to rely on an expert.

Bisphenol A (BPA)

The issue: Bisphenols are the chemicals that give us food containers, hard plastics, bottles and more. There are also troubling indications that bisphenols have carcinogenic and reproductive health effects, in addition to endocrine (hormone) disruptor capabilities, and they may also affect brain development in children. A recent study for the Centers for Disease Control indicates that bisphenols have been detected in the bodies of over 93% of the Americans surveyed. You'll find BPA in dozens of everyday items: water bottles, baby bottles, sippy cups and the linings of food cans, including baby formula cans. Most containers with BPA have the recycle **number** 7 on the bottom.

What to do:

- Start switching to BPA-free containers. Whole Foods and Trader Joe's carry a variety of BPA-free containers. Wal-Mart and plastics manufacturer Nalgene have recently agreed to phase out their BPA use. The US Congress and individual states have yet to take legislative action, but in 2008 Canada banned the use of BPAs in baby bottles.

- Limit plastics use in your home – see our kitchen section for tips on the categories of plastics. Bisphenols aren't the only bad guys you need to watch out for.

- Switch to glass storage containers – they're better for you, sturdier and cost around $20 in most stores for a 4-piece set. Also, thrift stores have great vintage glassware and Pyrex for just pennies. And take another look at your spaghetti and other glass jars; they're free and once you take off the label, they look quite nice as storage containers.

Arsenic

The issue: Arsenic can be found in water supplies, in some household pesticides and in pressure-treated wood – this includes outdoor furniture, decking, and home playground toys for children. You might even check your soil around these outdoor areas, as arsenic can leach into soil as well. Unless your outdoor furniture is made of redwood or cedar and has a **CCA-free** logo, you may have arsenic in your furniture or the soil in your yard.

What to do: Go to safe2play.org and order an arsenic test kit for $20.

Radon

The issue: Radon is the second leading cause of lung cancer in the U.S. Radon is a natural, radioactive gas that seeps into houses through cracks in the foundation or through well water.

What to do: Radon testing kits are available for as low as $10 through many national hardware stores. You may also call 1-800-SOS-RADON for more details on radon in your area.

PBDE

The issue: Polybrominated diphenyl ethers have been linked to behavioral changes, decreasing sperm count and hormone disruption, among other things. PBDEs are used in many household products for their flame retardant properties. The two main sources of PBDEs in homes are electronic devices and the foam in furniture. And in your mattress – more about that in Chapter 10.

What to do: Avoid non-natural foams and stuffing in cushions and mattresses. Look for natural stuffing like cotton and wool instead. When purchasing electronic devices, buy from companies that are phasing out or have stopped using PBDEs. A partial list includes: Intel, Sony, Ericsson, Panasonic, Toshiba, NEC, Hitachi, Apple, IBM, Philips and Motorola.

Phthalates

The issue: Phthalates are softening agents used in PVC products to keep them flexible and pliable. This chemical is most often found in children's toys and may leach (leak) out into the bodies of children as they put the toy in their mouths. Phthalates have been linked to cancer, developmental diseases and more.

What to do: Purchase non-plastic toys for your children. If you must buy plastic toys, look for toys made from non-chlorinated polyethylene or polypropylene – these ingredients should be listed on the toy.

Perchloroethylene

The issue: Perc is used in drycleaning and has been linked to cancer, birth defects and central nervous system damage.

What to do: Switch to a wet dry cleaner – wet dry cleaners don't use perc. If you can't switch, air out your dry cleaning away from your living space for a few days before bringing it inside and into your closet.

Formaldehyde

The issue: Formaldehyde is a suspected carcinogen and is a known respiratory irritant. Formaldehyde evaporates (called "off-gassing") from cushions, adhesives and other household materials. Conventional plywoods and particleboard in furniture and paneling contain formaldehyde adhesives, and the vapors build up inside the home.

What to do: Use cushions made from natural fibers and adhesives made from natural substances to help you reduce formaldehyde in your home. Be sure to keep your home well ventilated.

Mercury

The issue: Mercury exposure creates symptoms of visual impairment, digestive disturbances and neurological problems. Mercury is often used in thermometers, thermostats, fluorescent bulbs and lamps.

What to do: Switch out your mercury thermometer for a digital one – cost: $3.25 and up. Check with your state or local waste management representative for how to properly dispose of products in your home that contain mercury. Be aware that fluorescent bulbs should not go into the regular trash that goes to a landfill. DO NOT toss liquid mercury into the sink as it will make its way to your water supply and your surrounding environment.

Home Cleaning Products:
The Everyday Chemicals In Your Life

Now, what about some toxic ingredients in your cleaning products? You've probably felt the eye or lung irritation from tub cleaner or bleach – especially in a poorly ventilated room. Ever wonder why the stinging eyes and achy lungs? It is because those chemicals are interacting with your body – and your body is telling you about it!

To give you a better idea of some of the chemicals that lurk in your typical cleaning products, check out the list below – and then we'll discuss some more people-friendly and eco-friendly (and definitely **cheaper**) options.

A word to the wise: Chlorine and chlorine products are dangerous (acutely toxic), especially when used incorrectly and in combination with other chemicals. Three things to remember:

- **Do not combine bleach and ammonia.**
- **Do not mix bleach and acids.**
- **Do not use two drain cleaners at once or right after the other.**

Better yet, try chlorine-free bleach and avoid all the worries!!

FAQs On Household Toxins

Q: Where do all these toxins go when we spray or wipe them on our counters, our tubs and our floors?

A: They go into the air in our homes, into our lungs, on our hands and feet and eventually into our bodies, down our drains and into the water supply, out into the air around us, into the soil…you get the picture.

Q: What can we do to reduce toxins in our home and in our environment?

A: Most immediately, keep conventional cleaners and all other chemical products stored in a safe place, away from all family members and certainly away from children and pets. Start using green household products.

Toxic Ingredients In Your Cleaning Products

Chemical name	How it's used	What it does
Butyl cellosolve	All-purpose, window and other cleaners	Damages bone marrow, the nervous system, kidneys and the liver
Chlorinate phenols	Toilet bowl cleaners	Toxic to respiratory and circulatory systems
Denatured ethanol	Wipes & other disinfecting agents	Mucous membrane and tissue irritation, central nervous system problems when ingested or inhaled
Diethylene glycol	Window cleaners	Depresses nervous system
Formaldehyde	Spray and wick deodorizers	Respiratory irritant & suspected carcinogen (cancer-causing agent)
Nonyl phenol ethoxylate	Laundry Detergent & all purpose cleaners	Breaks down slowly into even more toxic substances
Perchloroethylene	Spot remover, used in dry cleaning	Cause liver and kidney damage
Petroleum distillates	Furniture and floor polishes, degreasers, all-purpose cleaners	Damaging health effects encompassing respiratory, nervous and other systems
Phenols	Disinfectants	Toxic to respiratory and circulatory systems
Sodium hypochlorite or sodium hydroxide	Household bleach, disinfectants	Can cause serious lung and tissue irritation, and can be fatal if ingested

The above information comes from seventhgeneration.com. Please visit their site for more about toxins in your cleaning products.

The Big Household To-Do List

(Short-term and long-term ideas for creating a less-toxic home)

Every item on the list below will translate into either direct monetary savings or indirect (but very real) savings in future health costs that you will never have to pay – or both. All of these will have a positive effect on the environment.

1. **Buy natural and non-toxic cleaning products.** Avoid cleaning products made from synthetic (man-made) chemicals. Buyer beware: There are no restrictions governing manufacturers' claims that their products are "green," "all-natural" or made from "natural ingredients." A company does not have to disclose all of the ingredients in a cleaning product, as that information is considered confidential to the company. Therefore, you may not have the full story on the specific ingredients in your cleaning products.

   Stick with all-natural and green cleaning products which are reputable and well-established. Also, when you look at the ingredient list (called the ingredient deck), do you recognize the words? In most synthetic cleaning products, the words look like a foreign language. Our thought is, if you can't pronounce it, don't use it. Most all-natural and green products will provide the scientific name and the common name so that people can recognize what is in the product.

Two Indoor Concerns

- Indoor air may contain between 20 to 150 different types of pollutants in concentrations reaching up to 40 times more than concentrations outdoors – much of them coming from typical household cleaners. (seventhgeneration.com)

- There are approximately 17,000 petrochemical products available for home use and less than 30% of these have been tested for their effects on human health as estimated by the National Research Council.

---

2. **Make your own cleaning products.** At-home versions of simple cleaners, like all-purpose cleaners, mold removers and air fresheners, are relatively easy to create and you can save lots of money. See how, below:

Cleaner	Typical Cost	Cost to Make at Home	How to Make	Level of Difficulty
All-purpose Cleaner	$3.50 average	$1.00 average	Make a paste of approx. 1/2 cup vinegar and 1/4 cup baking soda, or use diluted as needed.	Easy
Mold Remover	$3.99 average	$1.00 average	1 part hydrogen peroxide to 2 parts water. Spray on mold. Wait several hours, rinse.	Easy
Air Freshener	$1.50 average	$.75 average	Simmer water, lemon, cinnamon or other spices on the stove all day	Easy
Toilet Bowl Cleaner	$3.00 average	$1.00 average	Mix 1/4 cup baking soda with 1 cup vinegar, pour into toilet. Let stand for 10 minutes. Scrub with brush and rinse.	Easy

Please note that there are many variations of homemade green cleaning products out there, so experiment to see what works best for you. The cost savings are worth it!

3. **Air out your home.** Open your windows and doors at least once a week to air out your home. Your home is a tightly confined space when compared to the great outdoors, so toxins are present in a higher percentage. By opening the windows, you are allowing more clean air to circulate through your home, which is great for everyone.

4. **Take off your shoes when you enter your home and ask guests to do the same.** Simple enough, right? Removing shoes helps fight the battle for cleanliness, but it also stops chemicals you may be tracking in from entering into your home. Estimates by the professional cleaning industry say that up to 85% of the dirt in your home is tracked in from your shoes or your pets. *(healthychild.org)*

5. **Install a HEPA air filter in your home and consider air purifiers for high-traffic rooms.** Use air filters to clean up the air in your home. Check these out – remember that what you spend here will be spared in medical and pharmacy bills for allergies, general ailments and more. In a recent study, HEPA filters removed over 60% of particles from the air in homes and improved blood flow of subjects by 8.1%. (Feb. 2008 Journal of Respiratory and Critical Care Medicine).

6. **Install a HEPA filter on your vacuum.** Don't waste all your hard work when vacuuming – get some help from a HEPA filter to gather up more potentially nasty particles lurking around your home.

7. **Dust with a damp cloth.** Particles floating around your home eventually settle, usually landing on furniture and other items in the form of dust. A damp cloth can help "capture" these particles, while a quick dusting job simply sends them right back into the air in your home.

8. **Dispose of toxins properly.** You don't win any extra green points if you are replacing toxic chemicals with greener alternatives, but not disposing of the toxic chemicals properly. Take the time to do it right – batteries, light bulbs, car oils, cleaning products, paint and home repair items, electronic devices, paint thinner and pesticides, should never, ever go down the drain or in the trash. Find out how to dispose of them correctly! It's worth it to do it right – for you, your family and your community.

9. **Use cloth towels – not paper towels or wipes.** Cloth towels have less environmental impact than paper towels or wipes. You can also save money with cloth towels as they can be reused many times before being discarded or recycled into another use.

10. **Make large purchases that are good for the health of your home and the environment.** When purchasing furniture, bedding, rugs, mattresses and cushions, be sure to look for toxic-free options. Keep the toxic chemicals list in mind as you search

out your options. Feel free to look over our resource list in the back of the book for stores that sell natural options.

11. **Home improvement projects should have toxic-free living as a top priority.** Whether it be changing your carpeting or painting a room, do your research on toxic-free alternatives. Conventional carpeting off-gasses highly toxic chemicals, not to mention harbors many common allergens. There are many more environmentally friendly options including eco-friendly carpeting, sustainable hardwood flooring, cork flooring (a very affordable option for any family) and tile or linoleum. For paints, be sure to pick low-VOC and non-VOC paints. For more information, check our Room-by-Room Analysis chapter.

12. **Prioritize** – what can you afford to do immediately and what needs to wait until next month, next season or next year? Be realistic and stay committed to the fact that little changes over time make big differences – for your pocketbook, for your health and for the planet.

SOMETHING TO CONSIDER – Do You Bring Toxins Home From Work?

While you may do everything in your power to keep toxins out of the home, you may be missing an important avenue by which toxins find their way into your home – your workplace. For those who work with toxic chemicals (working in construction, medical, auto mechanics, manufacturing or in agriculture) or who have a combination workplace/ home (like a farm), see the list below for ways to keep those toxins out of your home. A USA Today investigation revealed that employees in over 35 states have unknowingly brought home toxins from work sites, exposing family members to such toxins as lead, arsenic, asbestos and pesticides. Heartbreaking, when you're trying so hard to do the right thing.

Drawing the Line Between Work and Home

The National Institute for Occupational Safety and Health suggests the following:

- *Leave soiled clothes at work and change clothes before leaving work*
- *Keep non-work clothes separate from work clothes*
- *Wash work clothes separately*
- *Store hazardous substances properly*
- *Keep family members away from the work area and away from hazardous materials*

nine

The Energy Vampires At Home

and how to slay them

Somewhere in your home lurks a vampire...but not the kind of campfire tales, scary movies, folklore and legend. This vampire may even be more nasty, as it sucks the very life out of your wallet and the planet. We're talking about energy vampires! But have no fear, let this be your guide to a vampire-free home! And as you root out the energy vampires, you will be a hero – not only to your family, but to the planet as well.

If you recall our U.S. carbon footprint statistics from Chapter 5, home energy use is the second largest contributor to the average American's carbon footprint, accounting for 36.2% of your total! In addition, most families pay over $200 a month in energy bills (a conservative number in parts of the country), with lower income families spending more than 20% of their budgets on home energy costs.

Where do our home energy dollars go? On average: 49% on heating and cooling, 13% on the water heater (!), 13% on our combined large appliances, 10% on lighting, 8% on small appliances, and 7% on electronics. Let's take a look at each of these parts of our typical energy bill and figure out where – and how – we can slay the energy vampires that are feasting on your budget.

HEATING AND COOLING – (49%)

Depending on where you live, heating and cooling costs may affect your budget differently. But with **49%** of your energy bill going into heating and cooling (regardless of the amount of your energy bill), this is a great place to start to reap big savings.

– 10 Simple Things You Can Do Right Now –

The following list gives you an idea on where to start, from least expensive to most expensive.

1. **Set your thermostat** – up 3 degrees in summer and down 3 degrees in winter. This can save you 1050 pounds of CO_2 emissions yearly, according to Global Green. Set thermostats separately for night use and for times when you will be away from the house for several hours. [🕯 and FREE]

2. **Make smart use of your shades and window coverings.** In the summer, close shades and window coverings to block out heat during the hottest parts of the day. Consider opening shades and window coverings in the winter (as long as windows are not drafty) to let sunlight and heat into your home. Think about investing in blackout curtains and other light-reflecting or light-absorbing materials. And, never forget the warming power of tea or the cooling power of an ice-cold glass of water! [🕯 and FREE]

3. **Replace air and heating filters.** While not always super-cheap, replacing these filters can shave much-needed dollars off your energy bill, which allows the entire heating and cooling system to run more efficiently, which ultimately equates to dollars in your pocket. Put a note on your calendar to check the filters every month, and plan to replace the filters every 3 months, especially during high-use months. [🕯 and $]

4. **Install ceiling fans.** Install ceiling fans in rooms where you spend significant time. Air circulation helps tremendously with keeping us cool – and using more fans instead of your A/C can reduce costs to cool your home by more than half! [🕯🕯 and $$]

5. **Plant some trees** – particularly on the west and south sides of your home. Why? One of the quickest, easiest and cheapest ways to minimize energy loss is to use Mother Nature's help. Trees will shade the home from summer's heat, and when they drop their leaves in fall and winter they allow sunlight back into the home – encouraging heat to enter and stay. This fix works particularly well on older houses that typically are less well-insulated and have more "energy leaks." Note: Unless you buy relatively mature trees and shrubs, don't expect to reap the full benefits of this one for a few years. [🕯🕯 and $$]

6. **Use quality weather stripping for windows and doors.** To test whether your window needs weather stripping, wet your hand and pass it over the window casing. If

you can feel air moving past your wet hand, then air is passing through the casing. Another trick: For doors, stick a dollar bill between the door and door jamb on the locked side. If you can slide the bill through, you need new weather stripping. If you live in a very cold climate, consider door thresholds and door shoes as well. [🌴🌴 and $]

7. **Check your insulation.** If your house is well insulated, heat will stay inside in the winter and outside in the summer. If you do not have wall insulation, consider putting in energy-efficient **green insulation** (such as recycled denim, recycled paper and hemp-flax alternatives). Make sure your installation expert is just that...an expert. Look for RESNET (Residential Energy Services Network) accreditation. Make sure they check for leaks before and after installation. [🌴🌴🌴 and $$$]

8. **Give your attic some love.** Or at least some insulation. Attics have the potential to leak a significant amount of energy. This also includes floors above garages, crawl spaces, etc., all potential spots where energy can be lost. Have an energy expert determine the extent of your insulation needs. [🌴🌴🌴 and $$$]

9. **Upgrade windows.** Look into double and triple paned windows made of wood or other material (preferably not aluminum, as it does not insulate as well). Low-E windows should be purchased with your local climate in mind; there are a variety of high solar gain, moderate solar gain and low solar gain options available. [🌴🌴🌴 and $$$]

10. **Assess your heating and air conditioning system.** A tune-up will keep your heating and A/C in tip-top shape. But what about for the long term? Is it best to just save up and get a new system...or is it more energy-efficient (and more affordable) to retrofit your current system? Make sure you use an expert to help you make the determination. [🌴🌴🌴 and $$$]

THE WATER HEATER – 13%

Water heaters are the second highest contributor to our energy bills. How can you keep your comfy hot water and shave a few dollars from your monthly energy bill?

– 6 Simple Things You Can Do Right Now –

1. **Conserve water.** Fix leaky faucets. Avoid washing clothes in hot water when possible. Don't let the water run. You've heard these a million times before, but how many times do you catch yourself brushing your teeth with the water running? Or automatically setting the washer to hot out of habit? [🌴 and FREE]

2. **Lower the thermostat** on your hot water heater to below 120 degrees F. Each 10-degree reduction saves up to 10% off your heating bill. If you live in a cold-winter climate and you can't imagine decreasing your water heater temperature in winter, consider a fall/winter and spring/summer temperature schedule. [🌴 and FREE]

3. **Limit baths and take short showers.** Don't want to? We completely understand! However, in many places, including southern Australia, water rations are a fact of life. Try to integrate conservation into your lifestyle, so that we won't ever have to worry about water rationing. [🌴 and FREE]

4. **Purchase low flow water fixtures** for showers, toilets, faucets and other fixtures. This simple step can save up to 50% of hot water. This is a relatively cheap way to make a huge impact on your energy usage and water consumption. [🌴 and $]

5. **Wrap an insulation blanket** around your hot water storage tank and pipes (especially pipes that run through unheated areas in your home). This can reduce heat loss by up to 40%, cutting your water-heating bill by up to 10%! [🌴🌴 and $$]

6. **Plan your next water heater purchase based on energy efficiency.** Look into tankless water heaters or solar hot water heaters. Each type of water tank – storage, demand/tankless, heat pump, indirect, integrated as well as solar – has specific advantages and disadvantages. The newest green trend is the tankless water heater – incredibly energy-efficient, especially when used in conjunction with low flow fixtures. Tankless heaters can reduce your water-heating bill by up to 50%. But do your research – each home's water heating needs are unique. [🌴🌴🌴 and $$$]

HOME LIGHTING – 10%

You don't have to live by candlelight to go a little greener and save a bit of green on your energy bill.

– 5 Simple Things You Can Do Right Now –

1. **Turn off lights** when not in use. We know you've heard it, but do you practice this on a regular basis? [🎋🎋 and FREE]

2. **Don't leave the light on** on your porch. Sorry, Motel 6. [🎋 and FREE]

3. **Switch to CFL bulbs.** The lifetime of a single CFL bulb can save over $30 in energy costs and save 2000 times its weight in greenhouse gases. [🎋🎋 and $]

4. **Buy Energy Star® qualified lighting and light fixtures.** They use up to 75% less energy, create 75% less heat and last up to 10 times longer. *(energystar.gov)* [🎋🎋 and $$]

5. **Look into solar or wind power and plan to get "off-grid."** Each region offers specific natural alternatives to electric power – solar, wind and water to name a few. Check out the resources you have available and budget what it would take to switch off the grid. This may take some upfront cost, but you are basically eliminating your home energy bill...forever! At very least, see what alternative energy options your local energy supplier offers. [🎋🎋🎋 and $$$]

SMALL APPLIANCES – 8%

These are our stoves, microwaves, ovens, coffee makers, humidifiers and other smaller household appliances. How can they be more energy-efficient?

– 4 Simple Things You Can Do Right Now –

1. **Unplug** smaller appliances (like your coffee maker) when not in use. [🎋 and FREE]

2. **Conserve energy** by maximizing your use of these smaller appliances. For your stove: Use the correct burner for pot or pan size. For the oven, check for proper functioning by testing oven temp with a separate thermometer. Use the microwave instead of the oven with smaller dishes – microwaves use up to 1/3 less energy. [🎋 and FREE]

3. **Purchase a power strip** and plug in appliances (like coffee makers, etc). Turn off the power strip when appliances are not in use. [🌴🌴 and $]

4. **Plan your next purchases around energy-efficient appliance models.** Consider induction cooktops, solar ovens, hybrid solar ovens and more. **Please note:** The Energy Guide Program does not currently provide information for stoves and ovens and the Energy Star® labeling program does not cover water heaters, stoves and ovens. Buyer beware on items in these categories that claim energy-efficiency – check for solid facts and figures that support the claim. [🌴🌴🌴 and $$$]

ELECTRONICS – 7%

These include your computer, iPod, cell phones, Blackberry, laptops, plasma TVs, TVs, gaming stations and much more. What to do to save energy?

– 6 Simple Things You Can Do Right Now –

1. **Putting your computer and monitor on sleep mode** could save you 80% of your electronics energy consumption and cut CO2 emissions by 1,250 pounds a year. *(epa. gov)* [🌴🌴 and FREE]

2. **Use those power strips.** As a reminder, many products consume energy even when they are off, and may account for 5% of your TOTAL energy bill. Use power strips and turn the power strips OFF when not in use. [🌴🌴 and $]

3. **Invest in solar chargers.** You won't be so dependent on your outlet! [🌴🌴 and $$]

4. **Consider a laptop** computer for your next purchase. Laptops consume on average 10% less energy than a desktop computer. [🌴🌴🌴 and $$$]

5. **Look for Energy Star® televisions.** Plasma TVs, while great to watch, use as much as 3 times the energy of their counterparts. If you can't live without a plasma TV, make sure you invest in an Energy Star® model. [🌴🌴🌴 and $$$]

6. **Look for Energy Star® computers** for your next purchase. Energy Star® computers consume up to 70% less electricity than non-Energy Star® computers. [🌴🌴🌴 and $$$]

THE WASHER AND DRYER – 6%

How can we get a few more dollars in our pocket and a bit more energy saved?

– 5 Simple Things You Can Do Right Now –

1. **Clean your lint screen** after each use to increase the efficiency of your dryer. Lint is also a fire hazard, so check this after each drying cycle! [🌴 and FREE]

2. **Wash only full loads.** Washing partial loads is wasteful in energy and water. [🌴 and FREE]

3. **Wash clothes on cold or warm settings, not hot.** For most laundry loads, warm or cold water is sufficient. When you use hot water, you are using over 75% more energy to heat the water. [🌴 and FREE]

4. **Line dry!** You can line dry on a drying rack in the house or on a clothesline in the yard or on the porch, and save precious energy and a bit of green as well. By the way, if you have to use a dryer – don't overfill it. That wastes energy too. [🌴🌴🌴 and $]

5. **Purchase front-loading washers and dryers or other Energy Star® appliances** for your next washer/dryer purchase. They hold more clothes per cycle, spin faster (which means it takes less time to clean and dry), use half as much water and can save you over $100 per year on your energy bill! [🌴🌴🌴 and $$$]

THE REFRIGERATOR – 5%

This is the single most energy consuming kitchen appliance in a home. How to put this little energy vampire in its place?

– 6 Simple Things You Can Do Right Now –

1. **Leave space between the coils** and your wall to allow air to circulate. [🌴 and FREE]

2. **Keep your coils clean** to maximize efficiency. [🌴 and FREE]

3. **Get rid of the extra fridge in the garage** and have one fridge that fits your needs. Be realistic about what size you need and get it. [🌴🌴 and FREE]

4. **Check your door gasket for a proper seal.** If your door doesn't seal properly, it's an "energy leak" at work! Gaskets can be relatively easy and cheap to fix. [🌴🌴 and $]

5. **Buy Energy Star® Refrigerators** – but for goodness sakes, get the size you need, not the biggest fridge out there! You could be wasting energy and money. [🌴🌴🌴 and $$$]

6. **Participate in Energy Star®'s "Recycle My Old Fridge" Campaign.** It's just what it says, a great way to unplug, say goodbye and recycle your old fridge. Go to energystar.gov to learn about their FRIDGE campaign. [🌴🌴🌴 and FREE]

THE DISHWASHER – 2%

– 5 Simple Things You Can Do Right Now –

1. **Air-dry dishes** instead of using your dishwasher's drying cycle. Using the drying cycle greatly increases your wattage and energy use. [🌴🌴 and FREE]

2. **Avoid using the pre-rinse and rinse-hold features.** These features are not necessary and add to your energy bill. [🌴🌴 and FREE]

3. **Wash only full loads of dishes.** The amount of water heated per wash cycle can't be adjusted, so make sure each load is full for maximum energy efficiency. [🌴🌴 and FREE]

4. **Buy Energy Star® dishwashers.** You can research the "Best of the Best" through the American Council for an Energy Efficient Economy's website (that goes for all appliances, by the way). You can check water usage on each model – models that use more water will be more expensive to operate than models that use less water. [🌴🌴🌴 and $$$]

5. **Consider a greywater system** to trap your dishwasher water for use in your garden. See page 98 for details. [🌴🌴🌴 and $$]

One Last Thought

It's tempting to focus on getting the big stuff (like solar panels or wind power), but it's essential to also keep your focus on the little things – the leaky faucet, drafty windows or other energy loss issues. You don't get extra green bonus points for making major expensive changes and then forgetting about the "little things." And it's those little things that often get our energy bill into trouble.

If you start following even a small number of the suggestions we outlined above, you can reduce your energy bill by **up to 50%** – a conservative estimate. And if you follow our longer-term recommendation to go solar and/or off-grid, you can count on a minimal or even non-existent energy bill. So start planning so you can save some cash, improve your health and support your planet!

ten

Room-By-Room Analysis for Healthy Living

> Home, Sweet Home! All this talk about toxins and energy vampires may leave you looking around at the rooms in your home, wondering how healthy and eco-friendly they really are. If you have questions, you're in luck, because I'm going to take you on a room-by-room tour and together we'll examine what it will take to move you into a newer, greener, healthier (and don't forget more economical) lifestyle.

BEDROOM

Let's assume you sleep six to eight hours each night – that's up to 1/3 of your life spent in bed! Most experts would agree that your bed could use some work when it comes to being green. **Here are a few ingredients in your typical mattress: PBDE's, Teflon, Formaldehyde, stain repellents.** Why are any of those bad? A couple of them – PBDEs and formaldehyde – should ring a bell from our chapter on toxins in the home. But let's take a quick look at them again and then discover some great, affordable options for your bedroom:

PBDEs – Polybrominated diphenyl ethers are used most commonly as flame retardants in a variety of household products, including your bed mattress. Concerns have been raised over the last twenty years on the accumulation of PBDE's in the breast milk of humans. Finding PBDEs in breast milk (along with lots of other chemicals) confirmed scientists' fears that this substance accumulates (adds up over time) in the body. The good news is that most mattress manufacturers claim they are phasing PBDEs out of their production process – but many don't have firm target dates yet. Also, remember there are quite a few types of toxic chemicals in your mattresses. (see nrdc.org/breastmilk/pbde.asp for more about PBDE studies)

Polyurethane foam – Here's where the formaldehyde is hiding, along with benzene, toluene and other bad guys. Polyurethane foam is the filling material in most mattresses.

Each one of these chemicals has its own tale to tell, but generally speaking, when these chemicals off-gas, toxic gases are emitted into our homes and the air we breathe. Many of these chemicals are proven carcinogens (cancer causing chemicals), teratogens (they harm embryos or fetuses) and mutagens (they make negative changes to our DNA). Greener alternatives to polyurethane foam include natural fillings such as organic cotton, wool and natural latex.

Eco-friendly Mattresses

What will it cost to purchase a healthier mattress? It depends (of course!) on what is considered eco-friendly. The least friendly would be your typical mattress ($500 and up). Next would be conventional mattresses not treated with PBDEs. Ikea has great and affordable options in this category, adhering to the strict European mattress safety guidelines ($200 and up). Ikea and other stores also offer futons for typically $300 less than their higher-end mattress alternatives. Often, futons do not use the same types of chemical fillers as mattresses – but be sure to ask! You can also find great variety in combination conventional mattress/organic mattresses ($900 and up). Finally, the most environmentally friendly and healthiest options are the organic cotton, wool and natural latex mattresses ($900 and up). [🏃🏃🏃 and $$$]

> ☞ NOTE: If you can possibly afford it, go for the greenest, highest quality possible – spending a little more up front to save on later health bills because of allergies or other effects of chemical-laden mattresses. But we're also realists and we know that once you know the whole story you'll do the best you can.

Organic sheets – If you can't afford a new mattress any time soon, consider purchasing organic cotton sheets. Depending on thread count, you'll pay $30 and up for a queen set. Organic cotton is now as mainstream as Wal-Mart, Target, K-Mart and Bed, Bath & Beyond. [🏃🏃 and $$]

Organic mattress pads – Organic cotton mattress pads are a bit more expensive than non-organic, but are well worth it if you can afford the extra cost ($150 and up for an organic queen pad, and $65 and up – but usually closer to $125 – for a non-organic queen pad. Standard pillowcases are made with synthetic polyester and/or goose down. Look for pillows made with kapok, buckwheat fills, synthetic-free latex, untreated wool or organic cotton. Conventional comforters and blankets are made with polyester and other synthetic substances, so look for wool and cotton alternatives. [🏃🏃 and $$]

Air purifiers – Since many items in the average home, including mattresses, off-gas harmful chemicals, you'll want to keep the air in your rooms as clean as possible. There are lots of air purifiers on the market – from single-room to whole-house – so you'll want to do some comparison shopping online before you buy. Remember, the unhealthy particles you breathe in interact with the cells of your body...why not aim for interacting with as few toxic chemicals as possible? [🌱🌱🌱 and $ – $$]

Houseplants – Add plants in your bedroom for a natural air purifier – and a lovely touch of green. All most plants need is just a little love. [🌱🌱 and $]

Clean your room! Your mom was right – you should clean your bedroom. A task as simple as washing your bedsheets once a week helps rid your bedroom of dust mites. Vacuuming and cleaning your floor takes care of dust particles, pet dander and other allergens. Make sure you investigate HEPA vacuums for your next purchase. [🌱🌱🌱 and FREE]

BATHROOM

> Two things to focus on here are your personal care items (for your health) and energy efficiency issues (for your budget and the planet).

Personal Care Products: Natural, "Natural" or Downright Unsafe?

It is hard to imagine that your lotion or shampoo could be causing you any harm. You might even take comfort in the fact that a label says "natural." **BUT**...loopholes in current US federal law allow manufacturers to **not** list all the chemicals that are in their skin care products. This allows a whole lot of questionable chemicals into your life – without your knowledge. Normal daily skin care regimens involve repeated small dose exposure of multiple chemicals over days, months and even years. We're only beginning to understand the long-term effects of small doses of chemicals that enter the body.

☞ *FACT: 1/3 of all personal care products contain at least one chemical linked with cancer. (data from Environmental Working Group)*

Chemicals and your skin: The skin is the largest organ in your body and it absorbs a significant percentage of what is put on it. Keep this in mind as you read down the following list of common personal care ingredients.

- **Parabens**

  Parabens are used as preservatives in food and skin care and are also known as "esters of p-hydroxybenzoic acid." Some common names for parabens include benzylparaben, isobutylparaben, butylparaben, n-propylparaben, ethylparaben, and methylparaben. You can often find these names on the ingredient list (the ingredient deck) of your skin care products. Parabens prevent the growth of bacteria in a substance (such as food or skin care products), but recent studies have shown a possible link between parabens and the development of cancerous tumors. *(from the Journal of Applied Toxicology, vol. 24, 5-13, 2004)*

- **Phthalates**

  Phthlalates are getting a lot of attention for their prevalence in many products – including skin care and numerous baby products. In 2000, the Centers for Disease Control tested 289 individuals and found that all 289 tested positive for at least seven phthalates in their bodies. **Every** person tested had levels of DBP (dibutyl phthalate) in their blood – with the highest percentage of this chemical found in our most vulnerable populations: children and pregnant women. Phthalates are hormone and reproductive disruptors and are not commonly listed in many products (those federal law loopholes!). Common culprits for this chemical include nail polish, hair spray, deodorants and fragrances; shower curtains, too, as long as we're in the bath. As a note, DBP and DEHP have been banned in the European Union due to safety concerns for humans.

- **Chlorine**

  Guess where? You'll find chlorine in women's sanitary products, especially tampons. This isn't good, since chlorine, a highly toxic substance, can be absorbed vaginally and enter the bloodstream.

- **Mineral oil**

  Mineral oil use in skin care has been criticized for, among other things, its "unbreathability" qualities, preventing the elimination of toxins.

- **Ethical concerns**

  Many major manufacturers test their products on animals, and a growing number of companies are abandoning the practice for more humane testing methods. If you have personal objections to animal testing, check out the products you use and see the company's policy. Numerous web sites can provide comprehensive product lists for you.

Buyer beware: Companies can label their products "all natural" or "natural" with little or nothing to support the claim, which means the consumer must be smarter than the product's marketing campaign. We highly recommend doing a little investigating on your own. Some good places to start:

The Campaign for Safe Cosmetics (safecosmetics.org) – If you're curious about companies that promote and agree to safer alternatives, look on this web site for their names.

Environmental Working Group (ewg.org) – For a report card on a favorite product or company, or if you just need to know more about a particular chemical on a product's ingredient list, check out EWG's Skin Deep cosmetic safety database.

Natural Skin Care Products – Some companies that have developed quite a following (and that you can trust) include: Hugo Naturals, Pangea Organics, Alba and Avalon products, Dr. Hauschka, Burt's Bees and many more. [🌴🌴 and $ – $$]

DIY – Don't forget, you can always make your own products, and for a fraction of what you pay at the store. A quick search at **wecanlivegreen.com** will show you lots of sources of information. [🌴🌴 and $]

YOUR GREENER, ENERGY EFFICIENT BATHROOM

Décor and accessories – Consider a few of these options: organic cotton or hemp towels and rugs. For toothbrush holders and soap dishes, try recycled glass products available online or in green stores near you. Look for natural toothbrushes and toothpastes and recycled paper products. [🌴🌴 and $]

Cleaning products – Use ones you make yourself (see Chapter 8) or products with planet-friendly, non-toxic ingredients. You'll discover that the results are just as good as with the old chemical-laden cleaners – plus no burning eyes or irritated lungs in the process! Seventh Generation has an extensive green product line, including paper goods *(seventhgeneration.com)*, and it's carried in many stores and chains. [🌴🌴 and $]

Faucets and filters – Low flow water filters and energy efficient faucets can save up to 3000 gallons of water per year. Consider purchasing new faucets and water filters for your sink, shower and bath so you're not wasting water. Make sure the filters also eliminate chlorine as well. If you're not ready to change out your old faucets, adding water filters to them is an economical and environmentally friendly way to go. But if you are tackling a home improvement project, check out faucets designed for energy efficiency. Even with the newer faucets, however, you'll still want to attach a filter to reduce chlorine exposure. [🌴🌴 and $$]

Leaks – Why throw water and cash down the drain? If you can't fix the drip-drip in your faucets, sinks and showers yourself, bite the bullet and call a plumber. The savings will come later. [🌴🌴 and $]

Toilets – Low flow is the way to go. A low flow model will use 75% less water than your typical toilet. The cash savings? Up to $100 a year. [🌴🌴 and $$]

Electricity – Simple savings: Use natural light when possible and install CFL bulbs. [🌴🌴 and $]

Water heater – Set your heater thermostat to a lower temperature. Keep in mind our water heater tips from our Energy Vampires chapter. Put a time limit on hot water usage in the home. [🌴🌴 and FREE]

KITCHEN

While some of us may feel this room is where we spend all of our time (and others of us may not remember what our kitchen is for!), the kitchen is where we can make the most significant changes towards a greener lifestyle.

Change how you eat. This is one of the most immediately effective "green" things you can do – specifically, integrating organic, vegetarian and "close to the source" foods into your diet and saying goodbye to processed foods. [🌴🌴🌴 and $]

Storage containers – If you are using plastic containers to reheat food…**stop.** Chemicals have been proven to leach into your food. Also, avoid storing fatty and hot foods in plastic storage containers – these foods easily absorb chemicals leached from heated containers. The best for you and the planet will always be non-plastic food containers, especially glass. But what about other storage options – like metal, ceramic and pottery, as well as wood containers? Often, these are not microwaveable like glass (be sure your glass containers are also freezer-safe and that you defrost completely before reheating). Buyer beware: If you purchase crockery (ceramics and pottery) made outside of the U.S., it could contain lead. Likewise, wood containers might have oils and/or finishes that are not safe for food storage.
[🌴🌴 and $ – $$]

Storage wraps, foils and bags – Most of our common storage items are made from plastic and petroleum-based products, and aluminum. These products do not biodegrade (break down in the land fill) easily, and they emit toxic chemicals in their manufacturing. Green options? Yes, but you may have to order online.

> **Can't live without Ziplocs?** Take your grandmother's cue and reuse Ziplocks as many times as you can. With a little TLC and patience, you might be surprised how long one will last. Actually, you probably would be surprised just how long a Ziploc does last...in the landfill, that is. A typical Ziploc bag takes thousands of years (and longer) to break down in a landfill.

For items that need foil or plastic wrap covering, consider **recycled foils and plastic wraps** found online at such stores as Greenfeet. For kitchen, garbage, lawn/leaf and com-posting bags, companies such as Biobag have created completely **biodegradable and com-postable** bag alternatives made of natural chemical combinations known as bio-polymers. This great new line of products can actually break down and return to the earth with little or no impact on the environment around them. [🌴🌴 and $]

Paper plates, towels & napkins – Want some affordable green alternatives? What about buying dishwasher-safe plastic "paper" plates you can use over and over? Better yet, look for bio-degradable and compostable disposable plates and utensils made from starch-based materials such as corn, potato, rice and sugar cane. They break down easily, are completely compostable and are made from natural substances. The bio-degradable items are slightly more expensive than standard paper plates. ($6.50 for a pack

> ### Eat Your Dinner (Plate!)
> Did you know there are edible (yes, edible...and biodegradable and com-postable) bowls, plates and utensils? They're currently being made by select companies in countries such as Japan and India. Just Google "edible dish-ware" and see what comes up!

of 50 at Branch Home online). If cost is an issue, keep a few eco-friendly paper plates on hand, and use your regular dinnerware as much as possible.

For paper towels and paper napkins, the most eco-friendly and cheapest alternative to date is to use cloths, towels and dishrags, and clean them as needed. If that just doesn't work with your lifestyle, consider reusable, biodegradable, compostable, chlorine-free bamboo towels from companies such as Luxe Bamboo. These amazing poker-chip size towels expand to an impressive 14" x 20" and are reusable and are washable as well. [🌴🌴 and $ – $$]

Dishwasher soap – Many name brand dish soaps are made with phosphates (comprising up to 9% of the total product), which get into local water systems and disrupt all organisms associated with these systems. Ultimately, chemicals in the environment affect us. Phosphates were phased out of laundry detergents in the 1970s, but have stuck around in dish detergents. Go figure. So, look for phosphate-free and chlorine-free detergents. We love Ecover, Mrs. Meyers and others. Pssst...you can also make your own dish soap to save a bundle! [🏃🏃 and $]

Homemade Dish Soap Recipe

> *2 cups of* **liquid castile soap** *(found at many natural foods stores and made of 100% olive oil), 2 drops of* **essential oil** *(your choice of essential oil if you'd like your soap with fragrance) and* **water** *as needed to dilute the mixture. That's it!*

Water filters: back to the tap – A great way to save money and help the environment is to drink water from the tap. There's a smart way to do this: First, you'll want to test your water for chemicals (test kits run $100-plus from websites such as Green Home). Next, purchase and use a water filter to filter out the chemicals you found in your testing analysis. Be sure you are getting the right filter for your specific needs. [🏃🏃 – 🏃🏃🏃 and $ – $$]

> ☞ **NOTE:** *When taking tap water on the go, don't put your water in plastic bottles, but use aluminum reusable bottles. Plastic bottles often leach Bisphenol A (see Chapter 8 for a toxins refresher course) and plastics should not be reused. Klean Kanteen has a number of aluminum bottle options available.*

Why Not Bottled Water?

*You may be thinking, what about buying bottled water? Mounting evidence suggests that bottled water may not be the best option. It may not test any better than the tap in your sink, so you are not necessarily paying for extra water purity. In addition, it takes tremendous energy and natural resources to make those bottles (plastic is typically a petroleum-based product). Used once and thrown away, they spend the next couple of thousand years in a landfill – probably much longer. And don't forget about the pollution created in the making of the bottle. Most recently, plastics have been proven to leak chemicals into substances, i.e., **into the water in your water bottle**. And you could be spending at least $20 a week for a family of four for the privilege! Isn't it more economical to buy a water filter and use your tap – saving money, improving your health and supporting the environment?*

Energy efficiency in the kitchen – Start with the simple stuff: Use CFL bulbs. Make sure your refrigerator is set at a more economical temperature, and that your fridge seal works properly – and that the whole family knows the "get what you need from the fridge and close the door" rule. See the appliances section of the Energy Vampires chapter for a complete energy-saving checklist. [🌲 – 🌲🌲🌲 and FREE – $$$]

FAMILY ROOM/LIVING ROOM

This is the place most of us long to be at the end of a hard day – kicking up our feet and simply unwinding. But this room, or any room where you spend a lot of time, could actually be costing you and your family more stress than relaxation. Why? The chemicals in your immediate environment.

Chemical sensitivities – This nearly unheard-of concept a mere 50 years ago has emerged as a cause of unexplained illnesses in families. People with chemical sensitivities exhibit strong physical and allergic responses to common chemicals in the home such as solvents, VOC's (Volatile Organic Compounds) in paints, perfumes, petrol, diesel and smoke – as well as sensitivities to pollen, house dust mites, pet fur and dander, and more. We know that many household chemicals are known to irritate our bodies when we use them, so it makes sense that some of us may be extra-sensitive to different types of chemicals.

Furniture – To combat chemical sensitivities, consider investing in non-chemically-treated furniture. Online stores such as Furnature (actual name) use no foam, vinyl, formaldehyde or other synthetics in their products. Many other green furniture stores use only natural oils, stains and varnishes to minimize chemical exposure to the consumer.
[🌴🌴 – 🌴🌴🌴 and $ – $$$]

Eco-friendly & Healthier Furniture Alternatives

Non-Toxic Paints

Any time you're painting a room, be sure to use low-VOC and preferably, non-VOC paints (Volatile Organic Compounds) – better for the environment and better for you and your health. Depending on the brand, there is virtually no difference in paint prices. Some low VOC and non-VOC paints are even cheaper than regular paints. [🌴🌴 and $$]

* **Recycled** furniture made from recycled products and reclaimed wood furniture made from salvaged wood. These can be great "character" pieces for your home.

* **Vintage** furniture (the fancy word for "used"). Continuing its life instead of trashing it adds up to big green bonus points. Just make sure you consider re-sanding or repainting with eco-friendly alternatives in the event lead paint or chemical-laden varnishes were used.

* **Bamboo** – This is considered a greener option due to its fast growth, but some argue that the chemicals used to alter the composition of the bamboo are too harmful to the environment and offset the benefits of fast-growing bamboo. Check into how the bamboo was manufactured and what types of chemicals, etc. were used to create the product. You might be better off with something else.

If You Must Buy New Wood Furniture

Look for **certified sustainable woods,** which come from sustainable forests. The Forest Stewardship Council certification (FSC) awards certification internationally to sustainable, managed forests used for lumber. But don't forget – you are still using trees for your furniture, and trees are becoming a rare and very valued resource on our planet!

Cleaning products – My best suggestion will always be to change out your cleaning and polishing products to greener alternatives. The cheapest option is to make your own. Next best is to purchase greener supplies. Examples:

- **Window cleaner** – Method Home's "Best in Glass" Cleaner in Mint, available at Target for about $4.00.
- **Kitchen cleaner** – Seventh Generation's "Wild Orange and Cedar Spice" Kitchen Cleaner for about $4.
- **Furniture polish** – Method Home's "Wood for Good" Furniture Polish for about $5. [🌲🌲 – 🌲🌲🌲 and $ – $$]

Room accessories – Organic cotton (or other natural fiber) furniture covers can help reduce your exposure to off-gassing chemicals from your furniture – but the effects are likely minimal. Consider purchasing a HEPA air purifier. [🌲🌲 and $$]

A NOTE TO THE HOME IMPROVEMENT CROWD

Whether you're fixing up to sell or just wanting to upgrade your home for the long term, you will be adding even more value if your improvements are green ones. Today, you'll find a tremendous number of resources for economical and environmentally friendly alternatives for flooring, cabinets, appliances, showers, toilets, shelving and more. Some of these improvements come with government tax breaks or manufacturers' rebates.

BUYER BEWARE... OF GREEN CLAIMS

As of the publishing date of this book, it is legal for advertising and marketing companies to make green claims on products that green experts would question. The reason: There is no set of structured guidelines in place on what is "green" and what is "not green." The FTC and EPA have developed a few guidelines to date, but more will be done over the coming years.

Savvy Tips About Product Claims

1. If a product claims to be environmentally friendly, determine if the claim is referring to the product, the packaging or both. If a product claims to be made from recycled materials, it must tell you how much of the product is made from recycled materials.

2. If the product says **"recycled,"** it must also say if it is made from "post-consumer waste" (items recycled after they are consumed or used) or "pre-consumer waste" (scrap items saved typically during manufacturing for later use).

3. When a manufacturer claims **"non-toxic"** or **"essentially non-toxic,"** they must be able to substantiate to consumers what they mean by non-toxic.

4. General claims such as **"environmentally friendly," "eco-safe," "green,"** and **"earth-friendly"** may make you feel good at the checkout stand, but unless the company can back up their claim with very specific information, it probably doesn't mean anything.

5. While the USDA Organic seal, the U.S. Green Building Council certification and the Energy Star® logo are a few certifications overseen by the government, currently there is no over-arching **green certification** process for green products. Be objective when analyzing claims and certifications – find out what the certification means and what organization supports the certification or claim.

6. For any product, look at the first several ingredients in **the ingredient deck**. Be on the lookout for the following "bad" words, especially:

   alkylphenol ethoxylates (APEs) – found in disinfectants and detergents; a suspected hormone disruptor

   ethylene-based glycol ethers (such as 2-butoxyethanol) – used in a variety of cleaning agents and a verified toxic air contaminant

   terpenes – found in pine, lemon and orange oils that are used in a variety of cleaning products

   sodium hypochlorite – found in bleaching and whitening agents

eleven

The Garage

tools, toxins and maybe a little junk

For some of us, the garage is a safe haven away from the hustle and bustle of our busy homes. For others, it's a catch-all room that we run quickly through as we park our car, for fear of junk-filled shelves falling on us. No matter which type is yours, it could probably use a little attention and improvement.

Organizing tips – Use eco-friendly organizational methods for tools, etc.: Before you go out and spend a bundle on organizers for the garage, take a look around your home, your neighbor's home, the local consignment shops and even the dump or salvage yard. Take a cue from your grandparents' generation that had a real knack for using items for a variety of purposes. A coffee can makes a great nail holder. Glass jars will beautifully display nuts, screws, washers and bolts. An unused terra cotta plant pot can become a stand, or a container for electrical, masking or duct tape. Salvaged shelving can be re-painted and mounted to the wall for tools and gardening supplies. You get the picture – get creative, get economical and make your grandparents proud! [🌴🌴 and FREE – $]

Toxic chemical storage – Keep your toxic chemicals (including the gas can) up and away from loved ones and pets. Until we can all move to a totally toxic-free home – and afford healthier alternatives – we'll need to be diligent about getting these chemicals safely out of the way, totally secure and locked. Make sure you've read all warning labels regarding what is acceptable to store next to what other ingredients. Be sure family members know this area is a "hands-off" area.   [🌴🌴🌴 and FREE]

Surge protectors and solar rechargers – Use surge protectors for all tools and appliances. Even your garage can be energy efficient! You probably have lots of things to plug or unplug in the garage, so do it right – and use your surge protectors. But be sure to turn them off again, to get the energy saving benefits. Also, research solar rechargers for tools you use often. [🌴 and $]

Electric mowers – Switch out your gasoline-powered lawn mower for an electric one. The cost is about $250 and up and the benefits to your wallet, your health and the planet are tremendous. If you have any type of respiratory irritation during lawn mowing, it could be related to the gasoline fumes you are breathing in – and putting out into the atmosphere. Some air quality management companies (check your listings for one near you) offer a trade-in of your gasoline mower for an electric mower for an astonishingly low $100. [🏃🏃🏃 and $$]

More on Mowers

Fuel cost per year:
Standard gas-powered mower: $20 to $50
Electric mower: about $3.

Carbon dioxide emissions:
Gas mower: 1 hour of mowing equals the emissions of
an automobile traveling 100 miles.
Electric mower: zero emissions.

Get rid of your junk. Goodbye to all that stuff in the garage that you don't really need. Why? It makes you feel better. It frees up space. It helps you adopt the "less is more" attitude. And you can give the stuff away to people who really need it – and be a hero! [🏃 and FREE]

RECYCLING
The Most Important Garage Project of All

Create a recycling center, with storage containers separating plastics from glass and aluminum, and a special items container. Depending on where you live, the concept of recycling is either a very easy or incredibly difficult task to accomplish. Even for states that actively support recycling programs, consumers still feel confused about "special care" items such as paint, light bulbs, pesticides, computer products, etc.

Many items can be recycled and there are very specific rules (that sometimes vary from state to state) about how these items must be recycled. As you progress with your recycling know-how you'll find that you will have less and less trash... and more and more recycling. It's a great feeling!   [🏃🏃🏃 and $$]

Plastics

Look at any plastic item and you'll see the recycling sign with a number and letters. The number refers to the kind of plastic and how (or whether) it can be recycled.

For example:

Here is a quick rundown on the meaning of each recycling number:

1 – PETE: Polyethylene terephthalate – Typically easier to recycle than other plastics. Don't reuse these items! They are believed to break down into two suspected carcinogens – DEHA and aecetaldehyde.

2 – HDPE: High-density polyethylene – A durable plastic used in anything from Tupperware to piping to snowboard rails, HDPE is often used for milk jugs, oil containers, shampoo bottles and toys. #1 & #2 plastics are the most commonly accepted plastics for recycling.

3 – V: Vinyl/Polyvinyl chloride (PVC) – A cheap plastic that permeates our homes in our piping, food wraps, vegetable oil bottles and much more. It is the second largest commodity plastic in the world and is considered by many environmental authorities to be **the most toxic plastic on the planet**. Experts advise against the use of this plastic – but be aware that it is used in almost every facet of your daily life.

4 – LDPE: Low-density polyethylene – A commonly used plastic for trash bag liners, produce bags, dry cleaning bags and cling wrap, #4 LDPE is generally considered more safe than other plastics (in addition to #2 and #5) for food storage.

5 – PP: Polypropylene – Used to make storage boxes, yogurt containers, food storage containers and more, it is generally considered a "safer" plastic: not yet proven to leach chemicals to humans, doesn't produce dioxin, chlorine is not used in its manufacture; often recyclable.

6 – PS: Polystyrene – Used to make disposable coffee cups, clam-shell take-out containers, disposable plastic cutlery and other take-out containers – polystyrene has been proven to leach styrene (a possible carcinogen and hormone disruptor) into food. Experts advise against its use.

7 – Other: Including polycarbonates and more, these plastics have come under recent scrutiny as studies have proven that a chemical in polycarbonates called Bisphenol A leaches into food, water and other liquids. Bisphenol A is often used in baby bottles, water cooler bottles, the linings of tin cans and some food storage containers. **Avoid this plastic.**

Your local recycling center can tell you what plastic categories they accept. Also, check on the rules for disposing of certain products, such as motor oil, pesticides and light bulbs. Until you're sure of your state's disposal policies, store your disposal and recycling materials in a safe place in the garage or another storage area. Some items **must by law** be disposed of in a very specific manner – which means *not* in the trash. For your safety, and that of your family and the health of your community and the planet, proper disposal of toxics is an absolute must.

A partial list of these items includes:

Appliances
Batteries
Brake fluid
Cell phones, PDAs, Blue Tooth, etc.
Chlorine
Computers and related office equip.
Conventional household cleaning products
Coolant/Antifreeze
Fire extinguishers
Gasoline
Light bulbs (any kind)

Mercury thermometers
Medicines including
   prescriptions drugs
Motor Oil
Packaging peanuts
Paint
Pesticides
Smoke detectors
Varnishes, thinners,
   paint strippers, etc.

The family that recycles together... Make recycling a family event. Post the rules and schedules in a garage location where everyone can see them. Think you might have better things to do with your family's time than sorting trash? Think again. By making time as a family to recycle, you are teaching through modeling (perhaps *the* most powerful teaching tool parents have), that taking care of your home and the planet is a priority. You are also teaching the **value of thrift**, as many recycling stations will give money for items turned in. We Can Live Green knows folks personally who have put their children through college by recycling aluminum cans. It adds up.

twelve

Greening Up (and detoxing!) Your Garden

All of us love a beautiful garden. We can spend a lot of time, money and energy to keep it that way. Ironically, many common garden practices have unintended consequences – like water waste, financial waste and adding to the toxic load in the environment. A few other not-so-healthy surprises lurk amongst your daffodils and daisies. Let's take a look.

☞ ***Water, Water...*** *If you're like most people, your garden accounts for 10 to 60% of your monthly water bill. As we move into a new era of water scarcity around the world and here at home, we need to know how we can still have our dream garden without wasting this precious resource (not to mention not using those chemicals that pollute our shared water supply).*

Matching your plants to your region – We've grown so used to planting just about anything that catches our eye and doing whatever it takes to help it survive, that we can lose track of Mother Nature's original intentions. Enough water, enough fertilizer, enough insecticide should guarantee a successful outcome, right? But let's say you live in a low-rainfall environment like Southern California or Arizona; perhaps it's not the best idea to plant a lush, tropical oasis that demands heavy watering.

If you want to conserve water, it's important to keep in mind the region you live in and the natural parameters given to you by Ma Nature. It may be time to take some of your non-native plants off costly life support – time to stop, take a deep breath, and see what actually *wants* to be there.

Drought-tolerant planting – Know your climate. If water is an issue, then focus especially on native, indigenous plants that actually thrive on neglect – those drought-tolerant species you don't have to water and they literally love you for it! You'll have a nice yard with a distinct variety of foliage, the plants are basically on auto-pilot, and you're spending significantly less money on watering and plant care. (For more on low-upkeep gardening, look into **xeriscaping**.) [🌳🌳🌳 and $ – $$]

Thirsty grass – The age of the lush green lawn may be coming to a close in many regions because of the growing need to conserve water. You might want to explore other, less thirsty, kinds of grasses – including species native to your region, and longer, softer grasses that need little water. Some of these don't need mowing as often! [🌳🌳🌳 and $ – $$]

Grass alternatives – Or do something entirely different with that patch of lawn, like create a rock garden or a meditation garden instead. You might even investigate artificial grass. This isn't your father's artificial turf from years back – fake lawn technology has made big strides lately, with amazing advances in color, texture and durability. However, it comes with its own set of environmental issues. Typically, it's made of polyethelene and rubber, so there's the potential for leaching of chemicals; also, measure the replacement rates of turf vs. real grass. On the other hand, the environmental issues with real grass can include chemical fertilizer, pesticides and water use, for starters. It's an option to consider. [🌳🌳 – 🌳🌳🌳 and $$]

Catching the rain – If you've got it, save it! Rain-catching devices can be anything from a bucket at the gutters coming from your roof or basins near the gutters with shut-off valves, to more elaborate systems that catch rain water in the ground through large containers. Find a system that works for you! [🌳🌳 and FREE to $$]

Greywater – One of the most overlooked and underutilized sources of water for the garden, greywater is the water that comes from your sinks, showers, clothes washers and dishwashers. It can be reused in the garden with no treatment (unlike water from your toilet – blackwater – which must go through a stringent treatment process before reuse). Greywater systems let you capture a tremendous amount of water that would otherwise go literally "down the drain." Some simple systems out there use conventional plumbing, others are more elaborate. Check your local ordinances regarding greywater – and look for tax breaks and other financial incentives that are sometimes offered in high drought areas. [🌳🌳🌳 and $$ – $$$]

Smart sprinklers –When you're installing a new sprinkling system, discover the new, smart line of sprinklers. When we say smart, we mean smart! They actually keep track of weather patterns, utilizing high technology to determine watering needs, and altering watering schedules based on recent weather and rainfall in your area. Some exciting examples include Aqua Conserve, Hydrosaver and more. Generally only available through irrigation and landscape contractors, smart sprinklers can save your household up to 40 gallons of water per day. [🌴🌴🌴 and $$$]

Hold onto the rain – Want to keep rainwater from being washed down the street and away from your garden areas? Check out smart pavers. They look the same as regular pavers and concrete except they are porous and breathable. Also referred to as porous concrete, permeable concrete, no-fines concrete, gap-graded concrete, and enhanced-porosity concrete, these products contain more porous space in their mixtures, which creates a drainage system for your rainwater to find its way into your soil, where you really need it. [🌴🌴🌴 and $$$]

GARDEN DETOX
(healthy alternatives for you and your plants)

What could possibly be going on in your yard that could be bad for your health? Well...chemical pesticides and artificial fertilizers, for starters.

Pesticides – While there are currently over 200 chemicals permitted for pesticide use in lawn and garden care, little is known about how many of these chemicals enter our food supply. The U.S. Geological Survey (USGS) states that over 90% of the fish in our rivers and streams contain common pesticide residue, and one or more pesticides are now found in waterways all across the U.S. These toxic chemicals persist in the soil and in our water supply for an undetermined amount of time.

Artificial fertilizers – There's not much good to say about them. Artificial fertilizers (the ones that you see advertised the most) place more chemicals into your environment and ultimately into your body. Some of their chemical components are known greenhouse gas contributors, and they are notorious culprits for degrading or breaking down ecosystems. Using artificial fertilizers can lead to an *increase* in pest populations, an overabundance of specific elements in your soil (including uranium) and can destroy the pH balance in soil as well.

So, forget chemical fertilizers and pesticides. There are organic, natural alternatives that really work!

ORGANIC, NATURAL & ALIVE

For fertilizers: Try organics such as fish emulsion, cottonseed meal, blood meal, manure and compost. **For organic pesticides:** Try bugs. That's right – **bugs!** If you have aphids or mites, invest in a ladybug population. If you have slugs, caterpillars or grubs, try ground beetles. They're called **"beneficial insects"** and you can purchase them online. Depending on the pest, you can also use non-toxic alternatives from plant sources such as garlic spray for aphids or vinegar spray for weeds. And while we're talking bugs, don't forget to stock up on **earthworms**. Red wigglers and night crawlers make a great garden team as they work to aerate soil, increase nitrogen levels and decrease runoff and erosion.
[🌴🌴🌴 and $]

> ### Worms 101
>
> *Having more worms in your yard can increase your plants' health and growth by 40%. Easy tip: Instead of purchasing your worm helpers, you can just add organic matter to your yard and the worms will come to stay.*

Composting – Composting is the process of creating your own rich soil amendment from your kitchen garbage (organic matter like fruits, veggies and egg shells) and degradable materials from your lawn and garden. Once you have started your compost pile you'll benefit from using worms (known as **vermiculture**) to break down your vegetable matter into wonderfully healthy soil, which you can spread around your plants to increase moisture retention and add valuable nutrients. There are many options on the size and details of your compost pile, but the end result will always be the same: You will save money, improve your health (fewer toxic chemicals in your environment) and support the planet (you are using the natural cycle instead of wasting all this nutritious stuff on the local trash dump). And your plants will love you!
[🌴🌴🌴 and $ or FREE]

Take It To The Bank

9 Best Household Strategies
&
Total Household Dollars Saved

1. **Do everything you can to reduce your exposure to toxins.** Reducing your exposure will benefit your health in more ways than you can imagine – in cost savings and quality of life. **The cost savings are simply too large and varied to adequately give a good estimate!**

2. **Consider making your own household cleaning products.** For a small investment of time and effort you will be supporting your health and the planet, while putting some cash in your pocketbook. **You can save $200 or more a year.**

3. **Reduce your energy consumption.** If you utilize any combination of suggestions from the Energy Vampire section, you can save up to 50% off of your energy bill. **Cost savings: a minimum of $600 a year.**

4. **Install curtains on your windows and doors.** Reducing the cold and warm air coming into your home can save you a small bundle. **Minimum estimate of savings for one year: $100.**

5. **Conserve energy and water.** Your water heater accounts for 13% of your electric bill, and 50% of your hot water can be lost to ineffective water flow. Best to save cash by fixing leaky faucets and installing low flow faucets, toilets and shower heads. **You can save a minimum of $150 a year – even more depending on your water usage!**

6. **Stop buying bottled water.** Purify your tap instead. There are a few exceptions to this, but if you purify your tap, you are getting equally pure if not purer water than most bottled water – all for a fraction of the cost. For a family of four, bottled water costs about $10 a week, minimum. **Over the course of a year, you can save a minimum of $400 – and you are reducing plastics in our landfills as well!**

7. **Plug your electronic devices into power strips** – that includes computers, iPods, TVs, DVD players, game stations and more! Power strips stop phantom load, which accounts for up to 5% of your energy bill. **Eliminating this problem in your household can save you a minimum of $100 a year.**

8. **Recycle...and get paid.** Through a little organization, planning and time commitment, you can actually make money by doing the right thing. Depending on recycling options in your community – and your family's commitment level – **you can actually make (at the very least!) $300-plus a year. Look into it!**

9. **Reduce your water consumption in the yard.** Reducing water usage can shave hundreds per year off of your water bill. **A 30% reduction in your water bill through water conservation (on an average $60 water bill) equates to over $200 in savings per year. And that's conservative.**

PART FIVE

At Work and School

The Goal: Expanding the scope of healthy living and energy savings beyond your home and into your workplace and school environments. Finding ways to involve other people in this goal.

The Reality: Organizations can be hard to budge when it comes to long-established wasteful or even harmful habits. You'll want to get others on board with your green ideas, so you're going to need some smart and savvy strategies (see below).

The Strategy: Demonstrating the potential cash savings and health & environment benefits of implementing simple (but hugely effective) changes in your workplace and school. Finding appealing ways of making eco-practices a part of your office or school culture. We've got 'em for you!

thirteen

Greening Up The Office & Classroom

> What do your workplace and your children's school have in common? They're both (probably) in buildings and they both probably use energy at a wasteful level. They may not have a recycling program yet, they use far too much paper, and the level of toxic chemicals in these closed environments is way too high. That's just my educated guess. But I know from personal experience that I'm not far off.

First, I'm going to give you some tips, guidelines and strategies that apply to both the workplace and the school, since a school functions as a workplace for its teachers and administrators. And then we'll look at specific steps we can take to make our schools healthier places for our children – at the same time as we're giving them vital tools for a greener way of life.

ENERGY
(and how to use it more efficiently)

Every time we plug something into a wall or turn on a switch we're drawing energy for our use. You might like to know where that energy is coming from. According to the Energy Information Administration, in 2004 about 40% of U.S. consumption was from petroleum, 23% from natural gas, 23% from coal and coal coke, 8% from nuclear power, and only 6% from renewable energy sources. So, until we're a lot further along in renewable energy availability, we'll need to be aware of the environmental fallout from our everyday energy use. There's no getting around it...for now.

> ☞ *In the United States, buildings account for over 70% of all energy consumption. So that's an obvious place for us to start looking for ways to conserve.*

7 Things You Can Start Doing Today

1. First things first...Do an energy audit. You need to know where your energy problems lie. You can hire an energy expert to come in to determine where you're losing money through energy loss and waste. You will also get suggestions on how to remedy these problems. Many utility companies will provide an energy audit **at no cost** to the customer. Once you have an idea of how much energy you're using, there are simple things you can do right away to start to bring the usage and costs down.

2. Power strips (the kind with surge protector capabilities) – Get them and use them. Turn them to "off" when your electronics are not in use. If you don't yet have power strips, be sure to unplug appliances when not in use.

> **Do Your Own Energy Audit**
> *(if this sounds like fun to you)*
>
> *Using the U.S. Department of Energy's formula for calculating usage, you can learn how much energy each piece of office equipment and lighting uses:*
>
> *Wattage × Hours Used Per Day ÷ 1000 = Daily Kilowatt-hour (kWh) consumption*

3. When to use "standby" – Standby mode for your electronics is a good thing, since it uses about 10% of the energy of the fully operational mode. But, at the end of the day, don't go off and leave everything on standby. It's still consuming energy. **Unplug** your electronics instead. Or turn off that power strip, once you get it.

4. Turn off the lights! Going out to lunch or meetings? You can save a lot of energy and cost by switching off the lights. Is it a sunny afternoon with nice natural light? Maybe you could dim the artificial lights or turn on fewer of them.

5. Change out the bulbs. There are many CFL and LED bulbs out there designed specifically for workplace use.

6. Create An Eco-aware Atmosphere At Work (Without Being The Bad Guy). I know of some workplaces that assign an energy monitor whose job it is to give support and encouragement (and definitely not to nag). You can leave "Congrats! You're saving energy!" notes behind with a small candy or gift card. For the unintentional energy vampires in your office, you could leave behind a funny note or card with a friendly reminder or statistic to get them inspired. You might also consider monthly contests or drawings to determine who has gained the most "energy hero" coupons for the month. To encourage workplace support of your new habits, consider a small prize or party for someone, or for a workplace team, who's been "caught in the act of conserving energy." When the savings mount up, maybe it's even time for some small energy performance bonuses.

7. Adjust business hours – If at all possible in your workplace situation – or if you're the person who determines the hours – consider switching business hours to match seasonal weather variations. For example, in cold winter months, employees could come to work later in the morning. This allows for roads to clear, but also allows for the natural increase in temperature to work with the heating system as the day progresses. For summer, earlier hours could allow employees to get out of the workplace before the heat of the day sets in. You can also dress warmer, or cooler and adjust the thermostat for additional savings. But you knew that one already!

A 4-Day Work Week?

When in Utah... *Can switching to a 10-hour, 4-day work week save significant money and energy? The state of Utah thinks so. Starting in August '08, 1,000 state buildings will be closed on Fridays, as 20% of Utah's state workers participate in a one-year pilot program. Other states and cities are watching closely and making similar plans.*

3 Intermediate and Long-term Energy Strategies

Once you've got your office or management team on your side you can really start suggesting changes that could cause a significant improvement in energy consumption. Many of these involve major purchases where the payoff comes later...but a big payoff there will be, for the company or school's bottom line and for the planet. (Plus, it might not hurt your standing in the company and you just might increase your chances for a raise!)

1. Alternative power sources – For many of us, buying alternative, renewable energy is just a phone call away to our local utility company. In some areas you may pay a bit more per kilowatt hour, but you are also driving the consumer market in the direction of renewable energy. This means it will become cheaper as time goes on. For the workplace, utilities expenses are **tax deductible**. It's also a golden public relations and marketing opportunity for bragging about your company's (or school's) greener energy choices.

2. Renewable Energy Credits – What are these? Renewable Energy Credits (RECs) help you to offset your environmental footprint and support renewable energy by investing in green companies and their projects. You can calculate your energy consumption via online websites or through an energy expert. You then buy RECs to compensate for your energy consumption. The most reliable source for RECs to date is Green-e, a non-profit group that verifies renewable energy credits to ensure their legitimacy (RECs are a new idea and not fully understood by many people, so there is the potential for "fake credits" to be sold).

Your primary focus should be on using less energy, **not** buying RECs only to compensate for your workplace's energy expenditure. Do your homework on the certifying body for the REC – they should be able to provide you with great references and credentials. When buying RECs, make sure you understand the project you are investing in – because you will essentially be helping to finance it!

3. Solar panels, etc. Of course, consider switching to solar panels and other renewable energy sources. We realize this may not be possible for many years. Keep abreast of tax breaks for your workplace investment in renewable energy and plan ahead! If a remodel is in your future, make sure you explore affordable, healthy, environmentally friendly alternatives.

Meanwhile…let's look at some smaller-scale projects where your workplace and school can get a lot of environmental bang for their buck.

5 Small Energy-Saver Projects

1. Energy Star® for office and school kitchen appliances – Energy Star® equipment for large and commercial kitchens includes reach-in refrigerators and freezers, hot food holding areas, steamers, fryers, dish machines and ice machines. If your office or work area isn't large enough for a commercial-sized appliance, take a look at the other residential-sized Energy Star® options. **The energy saved by these devices makes the appliance free after approximately two years of use.**

> ☞ **Buyer Beware:** *With Energy Star® it's important that you get the size that you need, as there are Energy Star® ratings for many different sizes of appliances. Buying **more** than you need basically negates what you are doing, by wasting precious energy – so be realistic!*

2. Before your next electronics purchase – Be sure to check out this fabulous purchasing tool: the EPEAT system (Electronic Product Environmental Assessment Tool). EPEAT simplifies the purchasing process for businesses and schools wishing to buy greener electronics. Supported by the EPA as well as many other participants, EPEAT allows purchasers to compare products based on environmental performance – such as reduction of toxic materials (like mercury, lead and more) within the product itself, how materials are selected, the ease of recycling the product, energy conservation attributes, "end of life" options available through the manufacturer, the environmental performance of the manufacturer, general information on the lifespan of the product and packaging information. EPEAT focuses on product attributes, not the rating of companies, and includes such products as laptops, desktop computers, monitors, printers, imaging devices and televisions. Soon, product attributes will also include servers, phones, PDAs and more.

3. When old technology dies – Be sure to recycle your electronics – companies like Motherboard will take your computers and refurbish them. Likewise, check with your manufacturer (if you use the EPEAT system they will provide you with this information) regarding their take-back policies. There are truly toxic components in your electronics devices and you do not want to put those in the trash because they will eventually come back to haunt you (literally).

☞ *Quick tips:*
  - *To reduce energy consumption, use software that takes up less hard drive space. Really know your needs.*
  - *If you're upgrading your system, don't toss your old hardware without good cause. Lots of potential environmental advantages to staying with your hardware.*

4. Office furniture with a past – Replacing furniture? Go for the used stuff. Salvaged/ Used/Consignment/Vintage all equate to the same thing: truly environmentally friendly furniture for your office. Why? With used, energy expended to make the product has already occurred, so you are not using new resources to create a totally new product. The quality of used products varies widely – but you can (and will!) find incredible quality furniture in your area with just a bit of research. See Chapter 10 for more eco-friendly furniture alternatives.

5. What about new furniture? If you must buy new, be sure the products have been created in a sustainable way. As mentioned in Chapter 10, for wood furniture check for FSC (Forest Stewardship Council) and Rainforest Alliance certified products. These organizations verify that forests are harvested in a sustainable fashion, which helps ensure the longevity and health of forests. Another great organization to become familiar with is Greenguard, which certifies companies that manufacture green products for your office and work place.

> *Caution:* Be sure you apply people-friendly and environmentally friendly paints and varnishes to your purchases. If you have an older piece, make sure the original paint did not contain lead.

RECYCLING

One of the best things you can do for the work place and school is to recycle. It's also perhaps the most time-consuming, depending on where you live and work. Recyclable items vary by region but include paper, cardboard, plastics, aluminum cans, glass and more. (Go back to Chapter 11 for reliable information on the types of plastics and other things most likely to be accepted in recycling centers.)

Recycling logistics – If you do not have recycling curbside service, you will need to set up a schedule with drop-off times, and this means **coworker volunteers** will do the drop-offs. It can be done! Next, you (or someone else in your office) will have to monitor the recycling within your workplace until recycling becomes as ingrained as any other daily task.

The payoff is huge and well worth the effort – both economically and environmentally. Workplaces, as we all know, tend to generate a tremendous amount of waste. Think of the paper waste in your workplace alone. Then, multiply that within your town, county, state, region and country – yikes! The great thing about recycling is that you are often financially compensated for your troubles, sometimes surprisingly well. Your workplace should discuss how to divvy up your recycling swag – an office party fund, a drawing for prizes, donations to specific charities, an end-of-the-year recycling bonus?

☞ **Good to know:** *Shred your used office paper, then recycle it – or use it as packing paper. You might be able to work something out with a local shipping service to do a trade/barter agreement.*

Eco-preneuring – If recycling is not readily available in your area, that means there's room for someone to start a recycling business. Why not you or your workplace or someone you know? Go online to find the many small business plans and resources for recycling businesses. You will be helping the planet and you could make some money along the way...sounds like a good idea!

How are we doing? The National Recycling Coalition's Conversionator gives quick statistics on your recycling efforts and how it helps our planet – these are great for finding fact nuggets for your work newsletter or to provide recycling inspiration to your fellow coworkers. Likewise, there are many Environmental Benefits Calculators out there that provide specifics on how your recycling and energy conservation efforts are helping the planet.

OFFICE PRODUCTS

Water: bottled or filtered, your cup or mine? Much has been written about what happens around the water cooler at the office, but what if there wasn't even a water cooler to begin with? Bottled water costs money and is typically packaged in plastic containers, many that contain BPA. Invest in a water filter instead and encourage coworkers to use reusable cups and plates. Put your name on your cup and you're good to go! For coworkers who bring bottled water or coffeehouse coffee to work, encourage them to use aluminum reusable water and coffee bottles instead of plastic – there is no BPA in aluminum reusable bottles. Simple steps to save a lot of money and waste. Many coffee shops will fill the reusable cup you bring in, and some might offer you a perk, as you are saving them money by not using disposable cups.

The best coffee – For coffee in the office, investigate "eco-coffee" – that is, coffee of the organic, fair trade variety. With organic coffee, you are assured of no pesticide residue and with the fair trade certification you can rest at night knowing that your coffee was harvested by workers who are treated fairly and humanely. Unfortunately, many of our luxury foods here in the U.S. come to us at great human expense. The most notorious food crops are coffee, tea, sugar and chocolate.

Cleaning products – For cleaning products at the office, go a bit greener or, as we've mentioned before, make your own green cleaning products. That goes for dish soap, dish detergent and hand cleaner as well. For eco-smart office supplies (from office cubicles, folders and storage centers made with no PVC, to double-sided printing machines (known as duplexers), pencils, pens, notepads and more), check out green online office supply stores such as Green Earth Office Supply.

Paper use (it's a real shame) – Paper consumption in the workplace and school not only exacts a high toll from the business owner and taxpayer, but it also exacts a tremendous toll on the environment. The U.S. actually consumes 1/3 of the world paper supply. Our paper use has tripled in the last twenty years and is expected to increase. However, forests and trees available for milling are decreasing at an equally rapid rate.

Paper...if you must – The only real solution to high paper use in the office is to digitize it as much as possible. But, if you must buy paper, buy recycled paper (and that includes recycled toilet paper, recycled paper towels, recycled napkins). Go for the highest percentage of post-consumer waste content you can find – the packaging will tell you. The higher the post-consumer waste content, the lower the likely chlorine content. There's chlorine in my paper goods? Yes, indeed, and it's bad, bad, bad for you and the environment.

Parting thoughts about work (not so applicable for school!) – Try to negotiate working from home, even if it is just one day a week – talk about saving energy at work! As we mentioned in our transportation section, speak to your supervisor regarding changing your work hours based on commuting and traffic issues in your local area.

AT SCHOOL

The "greening of our schools" is on lots of people's minds lately, and for good reason. Our children's health is precious to us, and when we say goodbye to them in the morning and send them off, we don't want to worry that their school environment could be a contributor to bad health. As a teacher myself and a new mother, I'm doubly concerned that we're doing the right thing. So, what's going on and how can we make it better – in terms of health, budgets and the environment?

Food...What Our Kids are Eating

School cafeterias definitely have their work cut out for them – how do you make healthy, nutritious food that appeals to kids and parents alike, all for an average of $2 a meal? Recent attention on the selection and quality of school lunch foods has helped to reform school lunches, but it's tough to change ingrained fast food habits. For example, while there are more healthy food options available than in years past (juice, apple slices and small salads have been added to many school menus), these choices sit next to take-out pizza and Chinese food, as well as other less health-friendly alternatives. You can imagine which food options the students pick first!

But some schools are going beyond simply offering healthier alternatives – they're totally eliminating the highly processed and packaged foods and returning to using local food producers and vendors. According to the Centers for Disease Control and Prevention, the number of overweight and obese children has increased by close to 20% in the last 25 years – due at least in part to our social focus on packaged, processed and "fast" foods. Schools are taking these statistics to heart and making some serious changes.

Buying locally produced foods – The benefits of buying local extend far beyond the health benefits for children or the financial benefits for adults and school systems – there are significantly more nutrients available in local food, versus food that has traveled thousands of miles. Childhood is a time of critical growth periods, requiring proper nutrients, but in today's food culture many of our children are eating **at their worst** nutritionally.

Harmless Additives?

Be sure to read the ingredient deck in any food your child is eating – and take the time to discover what those ingredients really are. Is everything with yogurt or fruit ingredients necessarily good for a child? Seemingly harmless multi-colored yogurt snacks, chips, fruit gelatin snacks, and more, carry additives that many experts believe can adversely affect a child's health. They can contain, among other things: sodium nitrite, saccharin, caffeine, olestra, and acesulfame K. Even more common are the artificial colorings (Blue 1, Red 40, Yellow 5, and many, many more) which laboratory tests have proven to increase risks for tumors, allergic reactions, to name but a few.

Waste…it's huge! Some of us at We Can Live Green have seen up to 100 full lunch bags of food thrown away in one day at one typical school. This accounts for a little over a **10% throw-away rate**, and this is not unique. It is difficult and disheartening to see money and food resources literally thrown in the trash. Help your kids realize the time, effort, resources and money that go into these products. I know that's easier said than done, but this is one issue that definitely starts at home, with the examples you set.

Toxic chemicals & green cleaning supplies – We are all familiar with the concerns over asbestos in schools, but a recent serious concern is about the cleaning supplies used in our schools, and their safety levels. As we mentioned in our household section, many conventional cleaning supplies have ingredients in them that may harm our bodies – like chlorine. Schools, and other institutions, typically use **institution-grade products** and that equates to higher quantities of chemicals to ensure the cleaning job gets done. Fortunately, there are equally effective green products out there. Organizations such as the New American Dream have extensive resources on green cleaning alternatives for schools. Likewise, organizations such as Green Seal certify green products for institutions.

Drinking water alert! – Water tests should be done regularly on all water sources at your child's school. A number of major U.S. cities have been alerted to problems with the water quality in local school systems. Example: In a recent study, the water at several Los Angeles schools was tested and found to contain unacceptable levels of **lead**. Lead affects the body negatively in many ways and appears to affect children's development in critical areas of the body such as the neural (brain) system, hearing and overall development.

HOW YOUR SCHOOL CAN CHANGE ITS ENERGY HABITS

School buildings consume a large amount of energy and you, the taxpayer, pay for it. With the nearly round-the-clock schedule of many school buildings, energy conservation must become a major focus for action. And since some schools are up to 100 years old and not built for efficiency, that can be additionally challenging.

Help from the top – Many schools have instituted energy conservation jobs within their districts, helping to direct the school and community focus on very specific actions to encourage energy conservation. But what if a school or school district cannot afford an energy expert? Then we've got to be creative and just dive in!

Starting from scratch – Someone (you?) needs to take the first steps by presenting to the administration a clearly defined set of guidelines for greening up your school. It shouldn't be hard to get them on board with you, especially if you can show how much money could be saved – or even earned – by starting a green program and involving the children and their parents. It's no longer a secret that wasteful habits have to change, and fast! Use some of the tips from earlier in this chapter and start to put together your plan. You'll want allies, but it shouldn't be difficult to gather a motivated "green team" around you.

Recycling…a win-win-win for your school – A well-organized recycling program can provide much needed funding to cash-starved schools. Recycling programs can teach students first-hand the importance of supporting their planet, while giving them a few lessons in economics as well. Best of all, it helps students take a personal interest in their school campus.

Time and money – In implementing a school recycling program, the most significant money investment for a school will be in trash cans for designated areas. The most significant time investment is to retrain students to place trash in the appropriate cans. Your school recycling program may be overseen by a specific department or club within the school or it might be overseen by the Parent-Teacher Association/Organization in your school. No matter who takes the program on, they will be rewarded – and with more funding for the school.

Paper waste – Schools are notorious paper consumers. How hard could it be to simply use less paper? Well…moving lesson plans, memos and homework to a more digitized format is challenging, especially if the school doesn't have generous technological resources. If your school isn't able to afford to move to a more digitized format, perhaps school funds can be used to purchase a **duplexer** (which makes double sided copies) and a paper shredder for used documents. Recycling paper waste should become a part of the school recycling program, and it gives back dollars for the effort.

SCHOOL GARDENS AND (yes!) WORM FARMS

We've already touched on the wonderful wonders of worms in your home garden, but what about a worm farm for your school? Worms have an incredible ability to make nutrient-rich soil from organic decaying matter. Why not save those cafeteria food scraps from getting stuck in a landfill and feed a few worms instead?

On to the garden! Once the worms have made the soil, what better way to model supporting the planet to our kids than starting a school garden? And then two things could happen: The school cafeteria can use the produce, or the produce could be sold at the local farmers market. (And you might have enough extra "worm dirt" to sell to a local nursery or at a community fundraiser.)

The benefits to your school:
- *a great educational opportunity for students*
- *the environmental support you are providing to the planet*
- *the potential for making money from the garden and the fabulous "worm dirt"*

GREEN SCHOOL CLUBS AND A GREEN CURRICULUM

Schools have a fantastic opportunity to educate students through green school clubs and general ecology education in the classroom. This can include simply planting seeds to watch them grow – which starts a great discussion on the importance of plants for our ecosystems – to more in-depth studies of particular topics. Green clubs have the potential to be the recycling center for the campus as well as energy efficiency experts for the school and community as a whole. Green clubs might also be in charge of gardening or other activities on the school campus that support the environment and encourage the school to save money.

BUILDING A GREEN SCHOOL
(you're not alone)

Green school summits are popping up all over the country, with huge attendance by vendors and school districts alike. The number of resources available for building a green school are astounding. The constraints of this book do not allow us to go into detail, but please check our website (**wecanlivegreen.com**) for great ideas. Ultimately, when schools save money we all save money, as we fund public schools. If your child attends private school, you are in essence funding that school too, so you have a financial stake in the greening of your school.

Take It To The Bank

6 Best Workplace and School Strategies
&
Total Workplace and Schoolroom Dollars Saved

AT WORK

1. **Reduce office energy consumption.** Saving energy equals saving money – so impress your supervisor and be a leader in making energy savings a priority in your workplace. **Shaving even $50 a month from the workplace energy bill will add up to $600 in savings by the end of the year.** It's easy to do, and that's just a minimum estimate!

2. **Go vintage.** When it's time for the office to get new furniture, encourage a vintage theme. Going vintage can save thousands...and there are very high quality vintage furniture stores out there! Example: If you compare a cheaply priced U-shaped office desk ($750 and up) to a vintage U-shaped desk ($400), it doesn't take long to see the savings add up. **That one vintage desk purchase alone could save over $350.**

3. **Skip the water cooler and go for the tap.** Water delivery services vary widely depending on the size of your office and where you live. Example: Compare an estimated $50 per month bottled water bill with virtually free filtered tap water (with the exception of the cost of changing out the filter from time to time and the initial purchase of the filter). **The savings? Up to $600 and more for one year.**

4. **Start a recycling club.** With budget cuts on the minds of many school districts, you can help your school make money by creating and running a recycling club. A great project for a PTA or PTO, Green Schools Club, or just a group of concerned parents, teachers and students. **Depending on the size of your school, your recycling club can realize thousands of dollars from recycling – much-needed cash in tight economic times.**

5. **Reduce consumption of energy, paper and other products.** Your school district will reap the benefits of decreased office costs, which allows more funding for other aspects of your children's education. **Eventually, these savings come back to you.**

6. **Encourage your local farms and actively promote more sustainable food options for your school.** Healthier food options for your children add up to **huge** long-term benefits for all of us.

PART SIX

Eco-Travel & Leisure

The Goal: Having the best possible travel and vacation experience at the least possible cost to the budget and the planet – without having to choose one over the other.

The Reality: Fuel costs are sky-high, air travel leaves a <u>huge</u> carbon footprint (not to mention cars), and green travel information is just starting to be widely recognized as an option.

The Strategy: Knowing where to go for the best information on traveling green, finding green lodgings and destinations. Knowing a few key tips for conserving energy and resources away from home. Getting familiar with the whole new world of green/eco-travel and its possibilities for adventure – while saving you money, minimizing your "footprint" and expanding your horizons.

fourteen

Ahh...That's Better!

budget-friendly, planet-friendly travel strategies

While we are one of the hardest working nations in the world, we still need to relax. In truth, most Americans don't spend enough time relaxing – many of us spend days, weeks and months in a never-ending whirlpool of work and personal obligations. "Relaxing" may include a trip a year to a destination of our choice, a weekly round of golf or the spa, or just sitting on the back porch to watch the sunset. Taking a moment to come up for air is seen as a luxury to most people, not a requirement for our survival.

I'd like to point you in the direction of some eco-friendly and economical travel and leisure options. Just because the evening news is troubling, it's no reason you can't plot your next escape.

Green Travel

How you get to where you're going is perhaps the most difficult aspect of travel when it comes to saving money and supporting the planet. Just getting there is the most expensive and energy-intensive part of any vacation or trip.

Getting There – To date, there aren't a lot of options out there for eco-friendly air travel and we are all familiar with the increasing expense of airline tickets, reflecting the cost of fuel. So what can you do? Limit your air travel as much as possible.

 Frequent Flyer Footprints – *A typical passenger jet emits about one pound of CO_2 per passenger for each mile it travels (statistic from Trees for the Future). Meaning that if you take a 2,000-mile trip you're responsible for releasing one ton of carbon dioxide into the atmosphere. When you consider how many of us are flying, and how often we fly, the emissions statistics are staggering.* (see Trees for the Future: treesftf.org)

Depending on where you live, you might be able to find a more eco-friendly way of getting to your destination. But with most American travel centering around fossil fuels (and then considering the price of fossil fuels), this aspect of traveling is incredibly difficult to make less costly on your pocketbook or the planet. With new technologies on the horizon, such as biofuels and other more economic fuel alternatives, the future looks a bit brighter for air travel. Until then, reduce your air travel if possible and consider carbon offsets for your traveling. Guidelines and regulations for carbon offsets are not well established yet, so do your research. But this is an option to lessen your travel load on the planet.

Green Hotels

Green hotels include any hotels (motels, inns, etc.) that are making greening a priority. How do they do that? Some may focus on conserving energy and/or water, while others make efficient use of the resources used by the establishment. Some have intensive recycling programs. A model green hotel should have a combination of all of these – and much more, from their landscaping to food choices to types of towels offered in your hotel room.

One of the first things you can do in your travels is to book your hotel stay at a green hotel. In the U.S., GreenHotels.com and others provide references to lodgings and their level of green commitment. I highly recommend that you also look at ResponsibleTravel.com, a U.K.-based full-service green travel provider featuring eco-friendly trips all over the world and accommodations that adhere to green principles.

But don't stop there – there are small steps you can take each day of your stay that will lighten your travel footprint's impact on the planet. Here are 8 for your consideration:

1. When you get to your hotel room, **unplug!** Unplug lamps and other devices that you will not likely use during your stay.

2. When you leave your hotel room, turn off the lights, TV, heating and A/C and other appliances you may have on in the room.

3. Ask the staff not to change your sheets and towels every day – or simply place the "Do Not Disturb" sign on your door. You can save a tremendous amount of water and energy by not having sheets and towels changed on a daily basis.

4. Check out the recycling program at the hotel – and support the effort while you're there.

5. If you open a bar of soap, take it with you to the shower and sink as well. Keep unopened amenities there for the next guest. Better yet, bring your own amenities. This will cut down on product packaging waste, and you will be assured the comforts of home. No need to lug around large shampoo and conditioner bottles – find small used containers in your home that you can use for your travel size amenities. Be creative!

6. Keep the thermostat at a reasonable temp – and if you really want to do the right thing, turn it down. Few climates in the U.S. call for Arctic temperatures in your hotel room.

7. When traveling in another country, ensure your water safety by investing in a **travel water filter**. If you have to buy water, be sure to buy a large container of water that is verified as <u>pure</u> and then use an aluminum or stainless steel reusable bottle for your daily needs. Or you can boil water to kill germs, but that may not fix polluted or chemical-filled water. There are chemical treatments available to treat water before you drink it (Aqua Mira, available for $13 to $18 and popular with hikers, treats about 30 gallons of water). Also, portable water filters ($50 to $300) can help prevent serious illness by eliminating disease-carrying microbes as well. Finding the right choice for you depends on where you are staying and what is available.

8. Influence your hotel by making suggestions on how they might improve (green) their services. If you are staying at a hotel with a less than stellar green reputation, your comments will go a long way. Remember, your consumer voice literally drives the economy.

Instead of a hotel – Consider shared housing. Organizations such as CouchSurfing.com and others help you find homes that are willing to take you in. In return, you open your home to them when they travel to the U.S.

Green Destinations

There are thousands of options here. Green destinations in general support a less consumption-heavy vacation, which equals less cash spent in the process. That's good news for all of us. A green destination may include walking or bike tours, mountain bike or cycling, wilderness trekking, river rafting, skiing, surfing, scuba diving, exploring natural wonders and much more (ResponsibleTravel.com is an excellent place to start your planning). Green destinations are usually cheaper than your average trip and you consume less stuff while making really great memories with your friends, family and loved ones.

Close to Home

Vacation options for almost all of us can be only a few hours away. We suggest focusing on vacations in nature, especially if you are trying to save money, but still want to enjoy a bit of down time. Nature is (almost) completely free to enjoy, is always there for you to enjoy and you will always walk away a happier person (with a happier pocketbook).

> ☞ *National park passes are just $80 for entry to all U.S. national parks. Senior citizens pay only $10 and if you are disabled, the pass is free.*

A few resources: L.L. Bean has a Park Search where you can access thousands of parks globally. The American Hiking Society and National Park Service also have extensive lists that are extremely helpful. Websites like Eco Travel, Family Travel Forum, the Access Fund and Green Concierge Travel are just a few resources to help you plan a greener vacation.

Bon voyage, wherever you're headed. Hope I've given you some tips you can use to make your leisure time a success in every way!

Take It To The Bank

Some Strategies for Your Next Family Vacation
&
Total Travel Dollars Saved

While this is a tough section to give solid dollar estimates for, due to individual variations in travel destinations and travel expenditures, here are a couple of "food for thought" suggestions as you make your next travel plans:

1. **Try a Vacation Price Comparison.** Not sure you can afford to travel this year? We did a price comparison for a family of four traveling two days by car to vacation at a major amusement park destination – and put those numbers up against the same family driving the same distance to vacation at a national park (we're not factoring in airfare here due to regional variations in prices, etc). Look what we discovered:

Amusement Park Vacation
(approximate average costs)

Gasoline (5 tanks for a 20 gallon tank) = **$500**

Hotel (2 nights on the road, 2 nights at the destination) = **$520**

Amusement park fees (2 adults & 2 kids, $100 per day) = **$200**

Food ($100 a day) = **$400**

Miscellaneous expenses (souvenirs, etc.) = **$250**

TOTAL: $1870 (Some would say this estimate is too low, others that it's too high. Do your own calculations based on your local amusement park attractions to find an accurate dollar amount.)

VS.

National Park Vacation
(approximate average costs)

Gasoline (5 tanks for a 20 gallon tank) = **$500**

Camping gear rental (if you don't already have it)

$100 for trailer rental for one week

$150 for basic camping gear, including tent, for 5 days (If you stay in a hotel, add $130 per night to your total.)

$50 for extra supplies

National park fees = $80 for an annual pass (for the driver and three passengers over age 16; children under 15 get in free)

Food (cooked by campfire or grill and bought from the store; packed lunches for the road) = **$200**

TOTAL: $880 (Some would say this estimate is too low, others that it's too high. Do your own calculations based on your local national park to find an accurate dollar amount.) **That's a savings of over $1,000.** And that's just one example. If you do more smart and savvy comparisons, I know you'll find your own eco-friendly (and wallet-friendly) destinations.

2. **Take the "One Tank of Gas Challenge."** We Can Live Green issues a friendly challenge to you and your family to find a suitable vacation spot that you can travel to on...you guessed it...one tank of gas. Get the whole family involved and see what destinations your family or friends come up with. When you agree on a choice, take the plunge and take your trip. Happy trails to all of you!

Afterword

Your New, Greener Lifestyle
a return to quality

And now we move on to the big picture. In this book we've discussed food and our homes and work and school and toxics and more. And we've looked at the enormous influence we have as consumers. So, how do all of these pieces fit together to make up the change we're looking for? In a word: lifestyle.

> **Lifestyle:** *A way of life or style of living that reflects the attitudes and values of a person or group. (freedictionary.com)*

Our lifestyle answers questions about who are we, what we stand for, what is important to us, and how our lives affect the world around us.

The media are giving increased attention to the emerging topic of a so-called green lifestyle. While initially viewed by some as frivolous – "Why are you talking about lifestyle when we're just trying to make ends meet?" – those addressing the issue are essentially hitting the nail on the head. Because it is through our *lifestyle* that we are improving or harming the world, changing or maintaining the status quo. A lifestyle may take a long time to change, but through consciously altering some of our old habits that aren't serving us well any more, we can find new ways of living – healthier, more economical, and far better for the planet we all inhabit together.

A Return to Quality

Lots of people would agree that our culture has been obsessed with "more, more, more for cheap, cheap, cheap." But this has not always been our national mantra. In years past, the focus was more on quality than quantity; quality was a measure of one's personal standing in the community. The gradual shift to a disposable, *quantity*-driven society started to occur about 100 years ago, and picked up speed, especially in the last 20 years. Over that century, disposable waste in the U.S. has increased 100-fold, the largest increase coming from "product waste," all the stuff we throw away. But, as we are discovering, there really is no such thing as "away" any more.

It seems to us at We Can Live Green that we're witnessing the beginnings of a true paradigm shift in our society. As we start to focus on quality, everything else falls into place: choosing the most environmentally friendly alternatives, having more money to use for much-needed health care or credit card bills or savings accounts, less waste generated as a result of fewer disposable products being created, fewer organizational issues in the home because there is less stuff to organize…and much more. Why, this kind of thinking could change the world!

Thriftiness is the New Sexy, Cool and Hip

Our grandparents' generation had it right: Save and reuse as much as you can, with no apologies. For a while now, thriftiness hasn't been a cool or even admirable quality. So now that we're convinced it's a good idea, how do we convince *others* that we are not "cheap," we're "thrifty," as we reuse our Ziplocs, garbage bags, rubber bands or string? That's up to you, whether you're the type who can offer a gentle lecture about carbon footprints, or you just tell your doubting friends to read this book, or you prefer to let your actions speak for you.

Getting Back to What Really Matters

We are all longing to do this. How many times have you said, "I wish I had more time to do what I really love" or "I never see my family and they are the reason I am working my tail off at work."

Three questions to answer YES to:

- Can I come to a place where I can make life fit my work and not have my work dictate my life?

- Can I get out from under the accumulated burden of an out-of-kilter, out-of-date lifestyle so that I can finally take control and move in a new direction?

- Can I envision myself getting off this hamster wheel where doing what I love (or spending time with those I love) seems like a special treat, not how my life should really be?

Yes, I know it's hard out there in the real world, and it's very easy to give advice. And I *know* it's tough to break old habits. That's what books like this one are trying to offer – a helping, understanding hand for the brighter road ahead. A greener, simpler road that holds out the promise of giving you and your family a lifestyle that actually works for you. And the best part is that a greener lifestyle works for *everybody*.

Mohandas Gandhi said, "We must be the change we wish to see in the world." No other quote speaks more powerfully of our own individual responsibility to start making changes in ourselves first...to "walk the walk." By doing so, we will change our communities, our nation and the world. Not bad!

I wish you my very best.

Jennifer

P.S. Come see us on the Web at **wecanlivegreen.com**. We hope you'll be a regular visitor, because every day we're posting new tips and resource information that can make your new green lifestyle just keep working better for you.

APPENDIX

Simple Science

Glossary

Resources & Product Information

Simple Science

1. Basic Biology (it's all about balance)

There are three basic categories of living things – **producers, consumers** and **decomposers**. Here's how they all work together in a balanced eco-system:

- **Producers** make their own food. Plants are the best example: They take sunlight, water and carbon dioxide (the gas that we breathe out every time we exhale) and make energy in the form of glucose. In turn, they "exhale" oxygen (giving us what we need to breathe). This process is called *photosynthesis.*

- Then a **consumer** comes along and eats the producer. That consumer (say, a rabbit) might get eaten by another consumer (a coyote).

- The remains of the rabbit that are not eaten by the coyote will be broken down by **decomposers**. Not a glamorous job, but someone's got to do it.

    Q. But what happens when the delicate balancing act among these living things is thrown off?

    A. Eventually, even a small imbalance can throw off the entire cycle of life. This is what is happening now to our global environments with such environmental issues as climate change, pollution, deforestation and basic habitat loss.

When a habitat is thrown out of balance, it is the organisms at the beginning (the bottom) of the food chain that feel the imbalance first. The living things at the beginning of the food chain are not usually that noticeable (think plankton in the ocean), so it's hard for us to imagine why it matters when unnoticeable organisms start being affected by an out-of-balance habitat. However, over time these small changes wind up making very big changes…and that affects all of us. That's where we are now, facing some very big changes on a global scale, and trying to find ways to return to equilibrium.

2. Your DNA: How Toxins Can Disrupt Your Body's Functions

With all the recent talk regarding going green and toxins in the environment, you may be wondering what it is about non-green products that are so bad for you. Let's go right to the source of the issue: DNA. DNA is deoxyribonucleic acid, and it is the blueprint for all life. It carries the instructions for every living organism to carry out its life functions. Your DNA is located within each of your cells and it tells the story of your body.

Decoding and "Reading" Your DNA – DNA is made of a sugar, phosphate and base. There are four bases (or building blocks), each known by a letter: **A** (adenine)…**G** (guanine)…**T** (thymine)…and **C** (cytosine). In various combinations, they make up all the codes possible for all living things. The only difference lies in how the "letters" (AGTC) pair up. In the DNA language, a "word" is made of 3 bases. One word might read: ATC. Instructions in the DNA language are very often more than one word long, for example: ATC GTA GGC. These words make a coded "formula" needed by your cells for protein. And proteins make a myriad of things for a living organism.

Uh oh… During the process of "translating" the DNA words, an organism can make a mistake. But fortunately there are repair enzymes whose job it is to fix mistakes. Even so, sometimes the mistake or "mutation" is not fixed and it results in a change in the organism. Mutations are not always bad: Think of the variety of life on the planet; some of that is a result of mutations – in fact, a whole lot of it is a result of that.

Mutagens – Mutations can be induced or speeded up by the presence of outside agents, called mutagens. These mutagens can cause a permanent change in the DNA. Who are some of these bad guys? UV radiation, cigarette smoke, asbestos and much more. Additionally, mutagenic substances are often also cancer-causing (carcinogenic). We are just discovering many man-made chemicals that cause a mutagenic effect on our DNA; we discussed some of these in our toxins chapters. This is why it is imperative for you to immediately reduce your exposure to chemicals and toxic substances. If you don't, you will be harming your DNA, the all-important blueprint for your life functions.

3. Basic Chemistry (a 2-minute primer)

Knowing a little something about chemistry will help with understanding the concept of carbon emissions, climate change and many other environmental issues.

First things first – Everything in the universe is made of **matter**...you, me, a leaf, your car's exhaust. Matter is made up of **elements**, more than 100 of them. (You can find the Periodic Table of Elements online.) The smallest representative part of an element is known as an **atom**, which has three main parts: protons, neutrons and electrons.

Atoms of one element often combine with other atoms of different elements to form **compounds**. Example: 1 atom of carbon and 2 atoms of oxygen combine to form carbon dioxide (the gas that leaves your body every time you breathe out). Another example: 2 atoms of hydrogen and 1 atom of oxygen combine to form water.

A **chemical reaction** occurs when compounds or atoms interact with other compounds or atoms. From their interaction, they create new compounds or atoms, as well as occasional energy, through heat, etc.

When chemical reactions occur, nothing disappears. This is due to the law of **conservation of mass**, which states that when a chemical reaction occurs, atoms are not created or divided or destroyed (therefore the mass doesn't change...hence the "law of conservation of mass.") This means that the atoms change form, perhaps even creating another compound, but that they do not, will not, can not just disappear.

Big deal, you may say. So, how does this relate to the environment? We're talking about stuff that we can't even see. Read on.

Relevant example: When a fossil fuel is burned (like petroleum), carbon dioxide is created through the chemical reaction that occurs. Remember, nothing disappears in a chemical reaction; it just changes. So when we use fossil fuels (and we're burning more than ever before), carbon dioxide is released into the atmosphere. Now, one property of carbon is that **it traps heat**. So imagine millions of cars, planes and factories running on fossil fuels, pumping out all that CO_2. No wonder our planet is warming up more than is normal!

4. Climate Change

Climate Change is occurring for two major reasons. The first is the emission of **carbon dioxide** gases into the atmosphere. The second is due to **deforestation**.

Carbon dioxide and other heat trapping gas emissions are caused by industrial processes (including power plants) and vehicles (including jets). The combustion of fossil fuels (petroleum, coal and other gases) are responsible for approximately 72% of the increase in heat trapping gas emissions globally.

And what about **deforestation**? The great forests of our earth have been likened to "lungs," because they truly breathe for us. They pull carbon dioxide from the atmosphere and they exhale oxygen. With massive global deforestation, you can see that we are losing our greatest allies in removing the excess CO_2 caused by our overuse of fossil fuels.

The chain of consequences – These heat-trapping gases do several things we are especially concerned about. Because these carbon gases trap heat, it only makes sense that the earth's temperature would increase. In fact, during the 20th century the earth's overall temperature increased by 1 degree Farenheit. That is the greatest increase in at least 1000 years!

Temperature increase throws off the natural balance of the planet. All of life exists within a delicate balance. Sort of like the fable of Goldilocks and the Three Bears...not too hot, not too cold, but just right. Every living organism must exist within a delicate perimeter of "just right" in order to survive.

What could happen with a "slight" global temperature increase? (3 scenarios)

One degree of increase doesn't mean one degree across the planet. There might be five degrees in one region and ten degrees in another. We are talking averages here.

SCENARIO 1. A slight increase can completely throw off an ecosystem's balance, killing some forms of life and causing other forms of life to become overabundant. Temperature changes can cause organisms to proliferate (reproduce) that typically would not have an opportunity to proliferate (think of more warm/hot months for mosquitoes to thrive and all the wonderful diseases they carry).

SCENARIO 2. An increase in temperature not only throws off the delicate balance for living organisms, it also throws off the balance of nature in general. An increase in temperature means an increase in water temperatures. This would create an **increase in sea levels**, as warm water takes up more room than cool water. It's called thermal expansion. Just as gases take up more room as their temperature increases, so do solids and liquids. One more thing: The higher ocean temperatures affect the frequency and power of storms, since tropical storms and hurricanes get their strength from warmer waters.

SCENARIO 3. With increasing temperatures, the melting of glaciers dumps more fresh water into the salt water of the ocean. This has a **domino effect**, causing stagnation (slowing down/non-movement) of the ocean, thereby affecting ocean currents. In addition to that, a change in the level of salinity (saltiness) of the ocean affects all organisms that are specifically adapted to living in a saltwater environment. Like everything else in nature, it's all interconnected. You affect one part of the environment and the rest of the environment eventually pays the price.

5. Fresh Water

Water is an essential element to life on our planet. Water covers over 70% of the surface of the Earth, with 97% of this surface water found in our saltwater oceans. Water fit for consumption by humans is known as **potable** water; water that is not potable can be made potable by distillation or chemical treatments.

Water scarcity in many parts of the planet is creating a growing social, economic, political and human health concern. In order for the human body to function at an optimal level, up to seven liters of water must be consumed each day – with a minimum of two liters per day to maintain a healthy body (depending on a number of factors including temperature, level of activity, humidity and more). By the way, drinking too much water can lead to a potentially fatal condition known as water intoxication.

Due to population increase and water pollution, the amount of available potable water has been shrinking in recent years. According to the World Water Assessment Program, the quantity of water available to all people across the globe will **decrease by 30%** in the next 20 years. (See UNESCO's World Water Development Report for more information) In addition, due to lack of fresh water we're seeing an increase in diseases related to contaminated water or drought.

☞ **FACT:** The United States leads the world in per capita water consumption: 70,000 cubic feet of water consumed per person per year.

As water shortages become more real, here and everywhere, it is essential that we conserve water any way we can. Conservation saves money, but more than that, it helps everyone on the planet.

6. Pollution

Pollution isn't good for the environment or for living things. Period. And there are a lot of pollutants out there. The major pollutants are in the air, water and soil. We also have noise, light, visual and thermal pollutions. We humans are very good at finding ways to pollute!

Air pollution (from industrial processes, transportation and other types of chemical reactions) – Air pollution's impact on the natural environment is extensive as it can kill many organisms. Its impact on human health varies from increased respiratory conditions/diseases, cardiovascular disease, throat and sinus inflammation, increased allergies and even death. Many nations have instituted guidelines for air quality to combat startling increases in respiratory conditions in humans, which most scientists believe are a direct result of air pollution.

Water pollution (from chemical spills, oil spills and otherwise contaminated water) – The impact of water pollution is felt by all organisms in an ecosystem, since clean water is essential to all living things on this planet. Its impact on humans includes disease, malnutrition, sickness and death.

Soil pollution (chemicals leaking into the soil through storage containers, pesticides, herbicides and others) – Soil pollution has several significant impacts on the environment. Soil pollution leads to a **breakdown in the food chain** because soil is host to many microorganisms which serve the beginning (producers) and end (consumers) of the food chain. Again, not a glamorous job, but these organisms sure are important! In addition, chemicals and pollutants in our soil end up in our water and food supply. They also spread to environments around them through storm runoff into rivers and oceans. In areas where high levels of soil pollution have occurred, we are now seeing "dead zones" where formerly healthy soil habitats have become lifeless – wreaking havoc on the delicate balance of nature in that particular location.

7. Population Growth – Crowded for Resources

The current global population is approximately seven billion. **7,000,000,000!** At no other time in earth's history have we had so many people on the planet.

You don't have to be a fancy mathematician to wonder about our limited natural resources and the ever-growing population and think, how can a planet with finite resources support a population that grows and grows and grows? The truth is, it can't, and many scientists predict frightening outcomes if we can't find ways for our planet to support life for this many people. Does that mean we should all stop having kids or hide our heads in the sand and wait for the end of the world? No. But we do need to look at our short-term and long-term futures and make some very complex decisions.

Everything in life has a cumulative (adding-up) effect. More people means demand for more space for houses, more food for nourishment and more clean water for drinking and sanitation needs. Not to mention the other "extra stuff" that most people want. Those things all come at a cost – to the environment. Because we live on a planet with limited resources, finding solutions will have to be a major focus of this century.

8. Why It's Good to Hug a Tree

Without plants, life as we know it would not exist. Why? Plants, through a process called photosynthesis, take the light energy from the sun and convert it into **glucose**. That may not sound that exciting at first, but glucose is the stuff that humans need to create energy for our bodies.

When we consume the plants, we take in the glucose and convert it to energy – and this energy is what runs our bodies. It is the "fuel" for everything we do in life. Even if we don't eat a lot of fruits and veggies from plants, plants still serve as the basis for our food supply. How? Plants feed the animals that we eat, and humans, in turn, eat those animals. The process simply isn't possible without plants.

But that's not all. Plants also give us **oxygen**, which we need in order to live. Remember the four necessities of life: food, water, air and shelter. Plants provide us with the air we need to breathe (as well as food....*and* water and shelter too if you think about it!). And we in turn provide plants with what *they* need to survive – mostly carbon dioxide. Plants take in carbon dioxide and combine it with sunlight and water to make glucose. The relationship is a bit more complicated than this, but you get the basic idea. It is truly an amazing process! Humans and plants have a perfect relationship – we both create what the other needs in order to survive. So, go hug a tree...that tree is helping keep you alive! Oh, and one more thing: That perfect relationship has gotten way out of kilter because we are now creating much more carbon dioxide than the earth's plants can possibly take in and convert.

9. Research and Statistics (and why they're so darned hard to understand)

Without a basic understanding of research, many statistics we hear about on television or read about in the paper are downright confusing and can even be intentionally misleading.

So, how do we demystify this mysterious part of science? We can start by understanding the basic purpose of research: Research serves to prove the effect of something on something else. The way in which research occurs is through an experiment. An experiment is a process by which a variable (the thing that varies) is tested to see how it affects something. For example: I give candy to half of my students before a test. The other half of my class gets no candy. The variable (the thing that varies) is the candy. Everything else is the same – the teacher, the room, the test, the class, everything!

An experiment is all about trying to figure out how something affects something else. There are other things to consider too: How big is the group studied? Are you studying two students or two million students? As you can imagine, the bigger the group studied, the easier it is to assume that observations made are a result of the experiment and not just random results.

The tricky thing about research is that sometimes results (and even the experiments themselves) can be manipulated or changed to obtain a certain outcome. That is why it is important for you to educate yourself on statistics and research as you go through your life. Learn and understand enough to not fall victim to poor research or manipulated results. Learn to see the truth behind the results!

Glossary

Biodiversity – The variation of life in a given region, typically used as a measure of the health of that ecosystem.

Bio-fuel – A solid, liquid or gas fuel that is created from biomass, typically referring to transportation uses.

Biomass – Living and recently dead material that can be converted to an energy source; most commonly used in transportation.

Carbon dioxide emissions – Gas emitted as a product of a chemical reaction. Carbon dioxide gas has a tendency to trap outgoing radiation from the sun, thus assisting in creating a "greenhouse effect."

Carbon footprint – The measure of the amount of carbon dioxide levels in the atmosphere, expressed in tons of carbon dioxide emitted.

Carbon tax – A tax on energy sources that emit carbon dioxide into the atmosphere.

Carcinogen – Any substance that is directly involved in the development of cancer.

Compost – The decomposed remains of organic materials; typically used in gardening, landscaping, and for soil erosion control.

Deforestation – The systematic clearing of forest lands globally, typically for agriculture, livestock, urban development or to use forest growth for paper products. Deforestation is the second largest cause of climate change, second only to carbon dioxide emissions.

Ecology – The scientific study of the abundance and interaction of living things.

Electric vehicle – A vehicle that utilizes chemical energy stored in rechargeable battery packs.

Fair trade – An organized movement that encourages fair labor practices, environmentalism, and progressive social policy for all people.

Going green – The social phenomenon describing individuals who use their consumer voice to increase sustainability and decrease human impact on the environment.

Green – A term commonly used to refer to actions that are environmentally sound.

Greenhouse effect – The effect of water vapor and carbon dioxide absorbing outgoing infrared radiation, raising a system's temperature. The term is generally used when referring to the Earth's temperature.

Greywater – Residential wastewater (from laundry, washing dishes and bathwater) that comprises 50 to 80% of residential wastewater. Greywater can be reused through various treatment systems to promote water conservation.

Hybrid vehicle – A vehicle that uses a mixture of two fuel sources. The most common hybrid vehicle today is a combination of battery charged power and gasoline-powered internal combustion engine.

Hydrogen fuel cell vehicle – A vehicle with an energy conversion device that creates electricity from the electrochemical interaction of fuel (hydrogen) and oxidant (oxygen).

Indigenous plants – Plants that are local and native to the region in which you live. Utilizing indigenous plants cuts down significantly on water usage, maintenance and upkeep in your yard or garden.

LEED certified – The Leadership in Energy and Environmental Design was developed by the U.S. Green Building Council to provide green standards for construction. Buildings can qualify for four levels of LEED certification, based on criteria found at www.usgbc.org.

Mutagen – Any agent that changes the genetic information of an organism. Mutagens are also often known as carcinogens: they promote cancer in addition to changing genetic information in a given organism.

Natural environment – The combination of all living and non-living things which occur naturally on Earth.

Organic – Products that are created or produced through natural processes.

Reduce/Reuse/Recycle – Reduce consumption of products. Reuse products when possible. Recycle all products that are recyclable.

Recycle – the process by which old materials are reprocessed to create new products.

Social responsibility – The belief that all individuals, communities, governments and countries have a responsibility to protect and assist each other and the environment.

Solar energy – Energy harnessed from the sun's solar radiation for purposes such as heating, electricity, transportation and desalination.

Sustainability – Human development that meets the needs of the present without compromising the needs of the future.

Toxics/pollutants – Compounds that are dangerous and have a poisonous, toxic effect on the environment.

Resources

Apparel
  Gaiam (www.gaiam.com)
  Nubius Organics (www.nubiusorganics.com)

Baby
  G Diapers (www.gdiapers.com)
  Green for Baby (www.greenforbaby.com)

Bath and Beauty
  Dr. Haushka (www.drhauschka.com)
  EWG's Cosmetic Safety Database Skin Deep (www.cosmeticsdatabase.com)
  Hugo Naturals (www.hugonaturals.com)
  Pangea Organics (www.pangeaorganics.com)

Business and Technology
  Green Technology Magazine (www.green-technology.org)

Cleaning Products
  Seventh Generation (www.seventhgeneration.com)
  Method Home (www.methodhome.com)
  Ecover (www.ecover.com)
  Mrs. Meyer's (www.mrsmeyers.com)

Consumerism
  The Story of Stuff (www.storyofstuff.com)

Energy
  American Council for an Energy Efficient Economy (www.aceee.org)
  EPA (www.epa.gov)
  Energy Star® (www.energystar.gov)

Environmental Sustainability
  Nature Conservancy (www.nature.org)
  Union of Concerned Scientists (www.ucsusa.org)
  Worldwatch Institute (www.worldwatch.org)

Green Building
  Global Green Building Resource Center (www.globalgreen.org)
  US Green Building Council (www.usgbc.org)

Family Fun
American Hiking Society (www.americanhiking.org)
Couch Surfing (www.couchsurfing.com)
Eco Travel (www.ecotravel.com)
Green Hotels (www.greenhotels.com)
National Parks (www.nps.gov)
Responsible Travel (www.responsibletravel.com)

Food
Fair Trade (www.transfairusa.org)
Farmers Markets and much more: Local Harvest (www.localharvest.org)
Organic Info: USDA Organic (www.usda.gov)
Pesticides: EWG's Food News (www.foodnews.org) and (www.ewg.org)
Vegetarianism: (www.ivu.org)

Health
Centers for Disease Control and Prevention (www.cdc.gov)
National Institutes of Health (www.nih.gov)
World Health Organization (www.who.int)

Informative Online Sites – General
Grist (www.grist.org)
National Geographic Green Guides (www.thegreenguide.com)
Treehugger (www.treehugger.com)

Kitchen
Biobags (www.biobagusa.com)
Compostable plates (search: bambu veneerware, bagasse)
Luxe bamboo towels (www.luxebamboo.com)

Lifestyle
Organic Spa Magazine (www.organicspamagazine.com)

Toxins
Pesticide Action Network North America (PANNA) (www.panna.org)

Water
United Nations World Water Assessment Program (www.unesco.org)

Work
Green Earth Office Supply (www.greenearthofficesupply.com)
EPEAT program (www.epeat.net)

Note: None of these companies or organizations has paid to be on this list. They are here because we believe their products and services will be of benefit to you.

Acknowledgments

A book is a labor of love – not of one person, but many. I would like to thank Paul Kelly of St. Lynn's Press for his perfect balance of encouragement and realism through this process and for bringing the message of the book to the public; Catherine Dees for her editorial vision, incredible patience and wisdom and unmatched wordsmith skills; Abby Dees for her expertise in legal advice; Christine Welch for her organizational skills and acute understanding of her field of work.

I am grateful to the following organizations for their research and dedication to a better planet: the World Health Organization, United Nations Educational, Scientific and Cultural Organization, Seventh Generation, the Environmental Working Group, The Natural Resources Defense Council, the Centers for Disease Control and Prevention, the National Institutes of Health, the National Research Council, the National Safety Council, the U.S. Department of Energy, USDA Organic, and The Environmental Protection Agency. And to online sites such as Local Harvest, Grist, Treehugger and National Geographic's The Green Guides for their straightforward and helpful insight on issues addressed in this book.

I would also like to thank my family – my dad for his steadfast optimism and support, my mom for her great creativity and English expertise and all that entails, my sisters for supporting me with kind words and love. Likewise, I thank George and Lynda for their gentle encouragement throughout this process. Most of all, I thank my husband, who serves not only as a hero to the public, but as my own personal hero for more reasons than I can count. Thank you for the beautiful life we have together and all the amazing memories we have yet to share. You are my everything, my inspiration, my joy and the reason that I wake up smiling every morning. You are the reason I am on this planet – thank you for the opportunity to share our lives together!

May this book help us all to make wise choices at this moment in human history so that we might help make this place we call home a better, healthier and more peaceful place – for all of us.

Jennifer Noonan can be contacted through the We Can Live Green website: **wecanlivegreen.com.**